[Marshal Deodoro and the Fall of Dom Pedro II]

CHARLES WILLIS SIMMONS

Marshal Deodoro and the Fall of Dom Pedro II

DUKE UNIVERSITY PRESS

Durham, N. C. 1966

Library of Congress Catalogue Card number 66-28493

Printed in the United States of America by the
Seeman Printery, Inc., Durham, North Carolina

To My Children: Lyn, Kay and Charles

Preface

Manoel Deodoro da Fonseca became the chief of state in Brazil following one of the longest and most peaceful reigns in the history of modern monarchial institutions. Dom Pedro II, the Emperor whom he deposed, had during his long reign justly earned for himself the sobriquet of "magnanimous," and his fall after a military revolt led by Marshal Deodoro was a source of surprise and dismay throughout the civilized world.

The need for investigating the background of facts which surrounded this military revolution and the importance of military disaffection in the fall of Pedro II has been suggested by a noticeable pattern found in many works treating the causes of the collapse of the Brazilian Empire. The conventional pattern of opinion has been that the emancipation of the Brazilian slaves in 1888 alienated the attachment of the agrarian aristocracy to the dynasty and led directly to the fall of the Emperor. Republicanism, religious conflict, and military dissatisfaction were other, but less important, contributing factors which led to the military revolt against the dynasty and the resultant development of a period of military pre-eminence in Brazil.

To Professor Charles E. Nowell of the history department of the University of Illinois who suggested the subject, and who has given helpful criticism, stimulating advice, and constant encouragement, I am indebted. I am also indebted to the personnel of the University of Illinois Library who have been uniformly helpful.

This monograph in its original form was a doctoral dissertation which I submitted to the history department of the University of Illinois. A considerable number of revisions and corrections have been made since that time. The translations in the text are, unless otherwise noted, my own. I take this opportunity to express gratitude to the librarian and administration of Virginia State College in Norfolk and to my wife, Margaret N. Simmons, for assistance and encouragement which made the revisions and corrections possible.

Table of Contents

[Marshal Deodoro and the Fall of Dom Pedro II]

Emperor and Empire, 1870

On December 2, 1825, three years and two months after the declaration of Brazilian independence, a son was born to Dom Pedro I, Emperor of Brazil, and to Dona Leopoldina, Empress of Brazil. This son, who was to become the second emperor of Brazil, was given the name Dom Pedro de Alcantara João Carlos Leopoldo Salvador Bibiano Francisco Xavier de Paulo Leocadio Miguel Gabriel Raphael Gonzaga. One year after the birth of the future Dom Pedro II, his mother, Dona Leopoldina, died. Dom Pedro was a sickly child, and two years after his birth a series of bulletins, indicative of the precarious state of his health, was published in the *Diário Fluminense*. The bulletins referred to the child's having been attacked by convulsions, but Alberto Rangel, in an article entitled ''A epilepsia imperil,'' published in the *Revista Nacional* in April, 1923, concluded that the appearance of this ailment in the second Emperor of Brazil in no way reduced his value or stature as a magnanimous ruler.[1]

Dom Pedro had been born in a time of troubles for his newly independent country. The republican revolution in the north had been put down during the latter part of 1824, and on June 14, 1825, the Cisplatine Province revolted and declared itself independent of Brazil. On November 24, 1825, the United Provinces of the Rio de la Plata declared the Cisplatine Province to be a part of their domain. Consequently, Brazil became involved in its first foreign war. The treaty of peace, which was signed on August 28, 1828, recognized the Cisplatine Province as the independent Republica Oriental do Uruguai.

The vast Brazilian Empire had almost 4,500,000 inhabitants and was divided into eighteen provinces, excluding the now independent Cisplatine Province. Except for the Banda Oriental, which had been under a military government, all of the provinces were governed by

---

1. *Revista do Instituto Histórico e Geográfico Brasileiro*, Special Volume, Part 1ª, *Contribuições para a biografia de D. Pedro II* (Rio de Janeiro, 1925), p. 46 n. The *Contribuições para a biográfia de D. Pedro II* will hereinafter be cited as *Contribuições*.

presidents who were named by the Emperor in accordance with the law promulgated in the Constitution of 1826. These presidents were assisted by local elective councils whose authority in the administration of the provinces was consultative only. The presidents of the provinces could accept or ignore the opinions of the councils. It should be noted that many of these presidents were men of exceptional ability; however, some of them took advantage of the poor communications and of their remoteness from Rio de Janeiro to exercise despotic government.[2]

The treaty of 1825, wherein Brazil's independence was recognized by Portugal, was very unsatisfactory to the Brazilian people, for Brazil agreed therein to assume a share of the Portuguese debt. This provision of the treaty increased the people's suspicion of their sovereign and aroused animosity against Brazilians of Portuguese birth. Another source of trouble for the empire was the conduct of its Emperor. Dom Pedro's mistress, Dona Domitila de Castro Canto e Mello, had borne him a daughter in 1824, but the Empress did not become aware of this fact until the following year. The Brazilian people looked with disapproval upon the conduct of the Emperor with his mistress, and when the Empress died on December 11, 1826, additional animosity was aroused when it was rumored that her death had been the result of a blow inflicted by Dom Pedro I.[3] Three years later, perhaps to still the gossip concerning Dona Domitila and following the advice of his ministers, Dom Pedro was married to Princess Amelia de Leuchtenberg, a daughter of Princess Augusta Amelia of Bavaria and Eugene de Beauharnais, a stepson of Napoleon Bonaparte.[4] The child Dom Pedro had little opportunity to know his stepmother because eighteen months after her arrival Dom Pedro I was deposed and Dom Pedro II, then not six years of age, became Emperor of Brazil.

Of this deposed Emperor who led Brazil to independence and who governed the country for almost a decade, Oliveira Martins observes that "descended from a European dynasty, a son of the Portuguese soil and not of Brazilian soil, he did not have in his blood, in his intimate soul, that essence of national spirit, that patriotism, the intimate fiber of the nation."[5] It is true that Dom Pedro I never relaxed his interest in Portugal, his native country. The death of

2. Raphael M. Galanti, S. J., *História do Brasil* (São Paulo, 1913), IV, 337, 338.

3. R. Walsh, *Notices of Brazil in 1828 and 1829* (London, 1830), I, 256.

4. Paulo Setubal, *As maluquices do imperador* (São Paulo, 1926), p. 140.

5. *Contribuições*, p. 131.

Dom João VI had increased his ties with that country, and his efforts to secure its throne for his daughter, Maria da Gloria, had aroused the ire of patriotic Brazilians. In the palace he had been encircled by a clique of Portuguese advisers. The demands for a liberal constitution had been ignored, and the failure of Dom Pedro I to heed these demands, along with the motives of the moment, led to his removal from the throne and finally to the formation of the republic in 1889.[6]

Two days after the abdication of Dom Pedro I, the children of the departed Emperor were brought into the city. They were under the supervision of Dona Marianna da Cunha Pereira, future Countess of Belmonte. The curious throngs of the city of Rio de Janeiro lined the streets through which the party passed and cheered the child Emperor who, following the instructions of Dona Marianna, smiled and bowed to his subjects. They went to the imperial chapel where, after the *Te Deum*, Dom Pedro II assumed the throne of Brazil. Later at the imperial palace, the members of the diplomatic corps were received and afterward Dom Pedro, from a balcony, received the joyous people and reviewed the imperial troops.

A few days later the Parliament nullified the decree by which the former Emperor had named José Bonifácio de Andrada e Silva tutor of his children. José Bonifácio, then a deputy from Bahia, in protest against this act published his "Protest to the Brazilian Nation and to the World." On the same day the Senate named as permanent regency the membership of the Senate and of the House of Deputies. On June 30, 1831, at a meeting of both houses, José Bonifácio was restored to his position as tutor of the imperial children. Later, on December 15, 1833, because of the political unrest in the country and of the suspicion of his pro-monarchial sentiments, José Bonifácio was dismissed from the position of tutor to Dom Pedro II, although his work in the education of the young monarch had in many respects been quite satisfactory.[7]

In accordance with the law of August 12, 1831, José Bonifácio de Andrada e Silva had nominated the following to instruct the royal children: Louis Aleixo Boulanger, master of writing, primary letters, and geography; Renato Pedro Boiret, professor of French; Simplicio Rodrigues de Sá, professor of drawing; Lourenço Lacombe, professor of dancing; and Fortunato Mazziotti, professor of music. Nathaniel

6. *Ibid.*, p. 132.
7. Mary Wilhelmine Williams, *Dom Pedro the Magnanimous* (Chapel Hill, N. C., 1937), p. 23.

Lucas instructed the young Emperor in English, and a relative of José Bonifácio, Alexandre Antonio Vandelli, instructed him in the natural sciences.[8]

The same decree which had ended José Bonifácio's tutorship made the Marquês de Itanhaen, Manuel Ignacio de Andrade Souto-Maior Pinto Coelho, the new tutor of the imperial children. The following year, after having been imprisoned and tried for conspiring to restore Dom Pedro I, José Bonifácio was freed by a jury and the old statesman quit the political scene in disgust.

The new tutor had always been a man of honor and integrity. He had been married four times and was sixty years of age when he was made responsible for the education of Dom Pedro and his sisters. In accordance with the law of August 12, 1831, he was required to present a report of his functions to the General Assembly. The report of May 15, 1834, contains some interesting information about the health and education of the young Emperor.

The Emperor, Senhores, has a weak constitution, and a nervous temperament. During last October he suffered an attack of cerebral fever which caused fear for his life. His recovery has been slow and interrupted by minor stomach ailments, but at present he is improving.

His education continues with amazing progress. . . . His Imperial Majesty reads and writes well, translates the English and French languages and also applies himself to geography, music, dancing and drawing; in the latter he has made admirable progress.[9]

On September 24, 1834, Dom Pedro I died in Lisbon. Since his abdication he had frequently written to his children in Brazil. The young Emperor, then nine years old, was deeply shocked by the death of his father. Their exchange of letters had kept them in close touch with each other. The old statesman José Bonifácio, in a letter of condolence, said to the youth, "They do not speak truthfully when they say that Dom Pedro is dead. Only common men die, heroes never die. They live eternally in the memory of the good, kind men who live after they are gone."[10]

During the regency Brazilian statesmen struggled desperately to

8. "Tracos biográficos de D. Pedro II," *Revista do Instituto Histórico e Geográfico Brasileiro*, CLII, 608-611; *Contribuições*, p. 68. The *Revista do Instituto Histórico e Geográfico Brasileiro* will hereinafter be cited as *RIHGB*.
9. *Contribuições*, p. 80; "Documentos referentes a infância e a educaçao do D. Pedro II e suas irmãs," *Publicações do Arquivo Nacional*, under direction of Commodore Frederico Schumann, XVII, 129-180 *passim*.
10. *Contribuições*, p. 81 n.

keep the country from disintegrating completely. Joaquin Nabuco refers to it as a "decade of political earthquakes."[11] Beneath all of the crises which overtook the empire during this period was the thwarted desire for local autonomy and even for the establishment of a republic. Until the death of Dom Pedro I, three factions struggled for control of the country. They were the Moderados, who later became the Conservative party and who were opposed to federal and republican sentiments; the Exaltados, who were federalists and republicans and who later constituted the Liberal party; and the Restauradores, who desired the restoration of Dom Pedro I. The disappearance of the last-named party did not simplify the task confronting the regency because, in addition to political friction, class friction was another source of trouble.

In 1834 the Ato Addicional was adopted to satisfy the demands of the Liberal party. This amendment to the Constitution granted elective legislatures to the provinces and provided a measure of freedom from the central government's veto. It also abolished the Council of State, an advisory body composed of imperial appointees, and provided that there be only one regent for the boy Emperor.

The regency of Padre Feijó and that of a Conservative, Pedro de Araujo de Lima e Silva, which followed the passage of this act did not satisfactorily quiet the unrest within the country. This led to the demand that Dom Pedro, despite a provision of the Constitution which required that he be eighteen years of age at the time he became Emperor and *de facto* ruler, be permitted to exercise the function of his office immediately. Mention had been made of the prospects of waiving this provision of the Constitution soon after the abdication of Dom Pedro I.[12] During December, 1835, Lima e Silva informed Dom Pedro that he would begin ruling at the age of fourteen, and urged him to prepare himself for the task.

In 1839 the Liberal party, in conjunction with a few Conservatives, began openly to sponsor the project of declaring Dom Pedro *de facto* ruler of Brazil. In the following year José Martiniano de Alencar founded the Club da Maioridade, whose mission was to give the young Emperor control of the state at once. The rapid progress which Pedro II had made in his studies encouraged the sponsors of the project. The members of this club boldly fostered the idea and

11. Joaquim Nabuco, *Um estadista do império, Nabuco de Araujo, sua vida, suas Opiniões, sua época* (Rio de Janeiro, 1897), I, 32.
12. Williams, p. 49.

through functionaries of the palace sought to get in touch with the Emperor himself.[13]

On May 3, 1840, two brothers, Antonio and Francisco de Paula Hollanda Cavalcanti, presented to the House of Deputies a resolution which urged immediate declaration of the majority and the resultant investure of Dom Pedro with supreme authority. The project, being a violation of the Constitution, was rejected, but it caused great excitement and Brazilians gave more consideration to the problem. In fact, the House of Deputies received a proposal that the Constitution be amended so that the young Emperor could be permitted to rule. This project was withdrawn only after the House had debated the question for two months.

The people of Rio de Janeiro, aroused, thronged the galleries during the debate in the House, and *vivas* for the Emperor resounded from them. It was proposed that a committee be appointed to consider and to report on the question of proclaiming Dom Pedro of age. Following the approval of the proposal, and confronted with the obvious desire of the people that Dom Pedro II be declared of age, the members of the opposition, mainly Conservatives, suggested that he be declared of age on his fifteenth birthday: December 2, 1840.

This proposal was strongly opposed by the Andrada brothers, Antonio Carlos and Martim Francisco, and by Antonio Paulino Limpo de Abreu, who demanded that the question be considered at once.[14] This demand caused violent debates among the legislators, and the regent, Araujo, called a meeting of Conservative leaders. At this meeting it was decided that the best solution of the problem would be to prorogue the legislature until late in November, and that the majority of Dom Pedro would become effective on December 2. Angry Liberals, receiving news of the dissolution of the legislature, stormed to the Senate and there, in conjunction with Liberal senators, authorized a committee of eight men to go to Dom Pedro II at Boa Vista. Antonio Carlos de Andrada, spokesmen for the committee, read the message, which requested Dom Pedro to save the throne and the nation by assuming office immediately. Dom Pedro requested that he be given a few moments to consider the proposal.[15] During this interval the regent, Araujo, and the minister, Rodrigues Torres, informed the youth of the plan for him to assume control of the country

13. J. M. Pereira da Silva, *Memórias de meu tempo* (Rio de Janeiro, 1896), I, 7.
14. José Francisco da Rocha Pombo, ''A maioridade, desde quando se cogita da maioridade,'' *RIHGB*, CLII, 220; Williams, p. 51.
15. Pereira da Silva, *Memórias do meu tempo*, I, 12.

on his next birthday. Advised by his tutors, Dom Pedro replied that
he wished to enter into the exercise of the function of the government
at once, and he revoked the decree which had prorogued the legislature.

On July 23, 1840, the following morning, the two houses met in
the Senate, and the Marquês de Paranaguá then declared that Dom
Pedro II had reached his majority and was in the full exercise of his
constitutional rights as Constitutional Emperor and Perpetual Defender of Brazil.[16]

The coronation of the Emperor was delayed until July 18, 1841.
It occurred in the Cathedral of Rio de Janeiro. However, before this
event took place, the first ministry which had been appointed on July
24, 1840, had fallen, and on March 23, 1841, it had been replaced by
a Conservative ministry. The fallen Liberal ministry, led by the two
Andrada brothers, had become extremely unpopular because of its
use of the spoils system. Antonio Carlos de Andrada, to secure a
Liberal legislature in the coming elections, had removed fourteen
presidents of provinces and other local officials and replaced them
with men of his party. Other undemocratic measures were taken to
insure the Liberal victory at the polls. These methods were successful
and the Liberals won a majority in the House of Deputies in the
elections of October, 1840. Such methods aroused indignation throughout the populated centers, and men of both political parties urged
Dom Pedro to dismiss the ministry. Thus, on March 23, 1841, in
compliance with the request of prominent Brazilians and following
the advice of his personal counselors, the young Emperor dismissed
the Liberal cabinet. The Liberal legislature was dissolved in May,
1841, and in the elections which followed the Conservatives won a
majority in the House of Deputies.[17]

Dom Pedro, at the suggestion of his advisors, asked that the
Council of State, which had been abolished during the regency, be
restored. This request was made in order that the young Emperor
could have available for consultation men of mature experience in
the government. The legislature granted this request, and on November 23, 1841, the council was revived. This council and the tutors,
Friar Pedro de Santa Marianna and José de Araujo Vianna, advised
the Emperor during the first years of his reign. On July 20, 1847,
the office of president of the council of ministers was created, and

16. Max Fleiuss, *História Administrativa do Brasil* (2nd ed.; Rio de Janeiro,
1922), p. 240.
17. *Contribuições*, p. 242.

thereafter Dom Pedro consulted the president of the council instead of consulting each individual cabinet minister.[18]

The internal disorder which had necessitated the declaration of the majority in 1840 continued until 1849. In January, 1841, Major Luis Alves de Lima e Silva, president of Maranhão, ended the disorders which had been prevalent in that province, and the following year he ended the disorder in São Paulo and Minas Gerais province as well.[19] He was then made Baron de Caxias and sent to Rio Grande do Sul, where a republican-federalist movement had been a source of disorder since 1835. Caxias, who now was the Emperor's strong man, ended this revolt in 1845. New troubles of a minor nature broke out in Pernambuco in 1848, but by 1849 Brazil's period of disorder and unrest was ended.

The problem of internal disorder which confronted the Emperor had been solved within one decade, but the problem of establishing and maintaining peaceful relations with other nations was to prove far more difficult. During the first half of his reign Dom Pedro II encountered various difficulties in preserving peaceful relations with England, Argentina, and Paraguay.

The difficulties with Britain stemmed from the slave trade. Stirred by the pleas of Wilberforce and other opponents of the trade, Britain had abolished slavery throughout her entire empire and had sought to influence other nations to do likewise. Portugal, a nation well within the British sphere of influence, had signed treaties with Britain for restriction of the slave trade before Brazilian independence. England had recognized Brazil and had persuaded Portugal to do likewise on the promise that the infant empire would end slavery within its domain. The treaty, which was to become effective three years after being signed, was to be observed for fifteen years. Little effort was made by Brazilian officials to enforce the treaty.[20] In 1831 a law was passed which provided immediate freedom for any slave brought from Africa to Brazil. This law also provided penalities which were to be imposed upon slave traders. However, the legislation was not enforced by Brazilian authorities.

When the treaty expired in 1845, Brazil refused to renew it. Britain, claiming that one clause of the treaty was perpetual, declared that all persons seized while engaged in slave trade would be regarded as pirates. The Aberdeen Act, passed during the same year, provided

18. Fleiuss, *Historia administrativa* . . . , p. 253.
19. Oliveira Lima, *O império brasileiro, 1822-1889* (São Paulo, 1927), p. 32.
20. Osorio Duque-Estrada, *A abolição* (Rio de Janerio, 1918), pp. 19-23.

for the trial of such persons in British naval courts.[21] British seizure of Brazilians engaged in the trade, the destruction of slave ships, and the entry of the British warships into Brazilian harbors to capture slave ships aroused the anger of the Brazilians and brought such a stream of protests that the two countries came to the point of war.

The growth of anti-slavery sentiments and the Emperor's personal aversion to slavery caused the passage of a law in 1850 which made the trade an offense of piracy. Rigid enforcement of this law ended the importation of slaves into Brazil. However, trouble continued with Great Britain, as she was reluctant to give up the influence which she had wielded in Brazil. During 1861 the "Christie Question" was a source of humiliation for the empire and caused Brazil to break off relations with Britain. This question grew out of the arrest and imprisonment of three drunken British sailors. When the authorities discovered that the sailors, in civilian clothes, were naval men, they were released. But Sir John Russell, acting upon the report received from the official in Rio de Janeiro, W. D. Christie, demanded that the sentry who had arrested the sailors be punished, along with the officer in charge of his post. He also demanded that the police chief and the commandant of the prison be censured for their treatment of the sailors. Christie was instructed to resort to reprisals should the empire fail to comply with the demands.[22] Demands were also made for payment of damages for the looting of the wrecked *Prince of Wales*, a British ship which had foundered on the Brazilian coast. Brazil's foreign minister, the Marqués de Abrantes, refused to accede to these demands, and British naval ships blockaded Rio de Janeiro. The young Emperor led his people through this crisis by accepting most of the British demands, but soon thereafter diplomatic relations were broken off with the British government.

The most serious external obstacle to peace was nearer to the empire than the troubles with the British. Juan Manuel Rosas, governor-dictator of Buenos Aires Province, in an endeavor to increase the size of his country and, incidentally, to recover a province which he considered a part of Argentina, had been awaiting an opportunity to intervene in the affairs of Uruguay and Paraguay. By 1843 Rosas, aided by a local political faction, the Conservative Blancos, was attacking the Uruguayan capital, Montevideo. Due to internal distur-

21. Alan K. Manchester, *British Preëminence in Brazil* (Chapel Hill, N. C., 1933), p. 244.

22. John F. Normano, *Brazil, A Study of Economic Types* (Chapel Hill, N. C., 1935), p. 92.

bances, Brazil was powerless for the moment to prevent the attack upon the capital, and only such aid as could be spared was sent to the beleagured city. The later establishment of order within the Brazilian Empire permitted more attention to be given to affairs of the Plata. Brazil, in an alliance with the Uruguayan Liberals, the Colorados, and the caudillos of the Argentine provinces of Entre Rios and Corrientes, defeated Rosas on February 3, 1852, ending his dictatorship.

Brazil's continued imperial activities in Uruguay in the form of loans and armed aid to the Colorados aroused the suspicion of Argentina and of the new Paraguayan dictator, Francisco Solano López.[23] López, some observers believed, had imperialistic aims of his own, and was fearful that Brazil's and Argentina's interference might halt his efforts at expansion. Anticipating a conflict with one of these countries, particularly Brazil, he built up a huge army. The continued Brazilian interference with the government at Montevideo caused him to center his resentment upon the empire.

In Rio de Janeiro, financial interests and the cattle barons of the Rio Grande do Sol area demanded further interference in Uruguayan affairs. The Blancos, who had meanwhile gained control of the government of Uruguay, were accused of persecution of Brazilian nationals,[24] and an appeal was carried to Dom Pedro to end the outrages suffered by his subjects in that country.

Recent elections had brought to power the Liberal party, led by Zacarias de Goes e Vasconcellos, and the new Parliament resounded with speeches demanding Brazilian intervention on behalf of its suffering nationals. In response to the pressure exerted upon it, the government sent José Antonio Saraiva as a special envoy to the Blanco government. Saraiva was to present Brazil's demands to that government.[25] Warlike gestures accompanied this envoy, troops being sent to the Uruguayan border and warships being ordered to its coast. Saraiva was instructed to demand the punishment of the chief offenders, payment of damages for property losses, and guarantees against further wrongs to Brazilian nationals residing in Uruguay. The Blanco government was to be informed that the troops at the border were there to prevent citizens of Rio Grande do

23. *Ibid.*
24. Pelham H. Box, ''Origins of the Paraguayan War'' (unpublished Ph.D. dissertation, University of Illinois, 1927), p. 108; Pereira da Silva, *Memórias do meu tempo*, II, 7, 8; Normano, *Brazil, A Study of Economic Types*, p. 92; Nabuco, *Um estadista do empério*, II, 165.
25. Box, p. 121.

Sul from aiding the Colorados or to protect lives, honor, and property of Brazilians in Uruguay, should the Blanco government be unable to protect them.

Aguirre, the new Blanco caudillo, had turned to López of Paraguay for protection against the encroachments of Brazil. Saraiva, on arrival in Montevideo, recognized the danger inherent in the situation, and he, making no allusion to the possible use of Brazilian troops, presented only a part of his government's demands.[26] Receiving no satisfaction, he turned for support to Argentina, which likewise had claims against the Uruguayan government. In conjunction with the minister of Argentina and the British minister, who was a neutral in the affair, they conferred with Aguirre, the Blanco president of Uruguay. This method also failed to meet with success. Saraiva then sought Argentine aid to force the factions to lay down their arms. Mitre, president of Argentina, would not agree to this, but he was willing to have Brazil undertake the task without Argentine aid.

When the Zacarias ministry was informed of Mitre's attitude, Saraiva was instructed to present an ultimatum to the Uruguayan government. Six weeks later, on September 14, 1864, Brazilian troops invaded Uruguay. López, to whom Aguirre had turned for aid, twice protested against Brazil's action, and after the invasion of Uruguay he acted to prevent this ''attack upon the balance of power of the Plata states.''[27] The Brazilian steamship *Marquês de Olinda*, on its way to Mato Grosso on the Paraguay River and carrying the new president of Mato Grosso Province, was captured by Paraguayan military forces. After this act of aggression the Brazilian government was informed that the river was closed to Brazilian vessels and that diplomatic relations were broken off between the two countries. López, in December, 1864, ordered elements of the armed forces to invade Mato Grosso. In the war that followed, after bitter and protracted fighting, López was killed and his army defeated. The official date of the war's ending was March 1, 1870.[28]

The Paraguayan War deeply affected the evolution of the various political parties and the political and social development of the entire nation of Brazil. During the years in which the conflict was in progress there was continuous evidence of loss of prestige for the dynasty, tacit opposition by the army and by the navy, and a growing coolness

26. Pereira da Silva, *Memórias do meu tempo*, II, 11.
27. *Ibid.*, p. 14; Box, p. 217.
28. *Jornal do Comércio*, Edição Comemorativa do 1º Centenário da Independência do Brasil, 1822-1922 (Sept. 7, 1922), p. 308.

between the monarchy and clergy.[29] The historian Calogeras considers the transformation to be the result of Brazil's Constitution, which had, in addition to the customary executive, legislative, and judicial powers, a fourth division of power—the moderative. This latter power required that the emperor "watch incessantly over the maintenance of the independence, equilibrium, and harmony of the rest of the political powers." It permitted Dom Pedro II to exercise final authority in directing the affairs of Brazil. Ministries held office at his pleasure, and he could and did, on occasion, replace a ministry with the knowledge that the new ministry would have little difficulty in obtaining a majority in the House of Deputies at the next election. The moderative power will receive additional attention in the following pages, but it should be noted that many of the troubles which beset the empire during the last years of Dom Pedro's reign are possibly traceable to other causes of more importance than the *poder moderador* of the Constitution.

During the period of the Paraguayan War and the decade which followed it, Dom Pedro's prestige and power awed many foreigners. An American who visited Brazil during this time wrote as follows: "The appearance of the Emperor was impressive: his physique was magnificent, upwards of six feet in height, and finely proportioned; his head well developed, and his intellectual face expressive of generous qualities, give him an air of distinction."[30] At the same time that Brazil was blessed with this vigorous and intelligent Emperor, she was also fortunate to have outstanding men in politics, diplomacy, and the armed forces. All of them were moved by intense patriotism and were unified under the prudent direction of the Emperor, "in whom was enshrined the sentiments of the nation during this national emergency."[31]

The Emperor, who was aware of his power, knew the politics of his country better than any man. When he was faced by the opposition of Liberals and Republicans during this period of crisis, he, magnanimous of heart, highly cultured in spirit, and incapable of using violence, systematically resorted to the use of the *poder moderador* as a means of consolidating his dynasty.[32] Such a solution of the

29. João Pandiá Calogeras, *History of Brazil*, ed. and trans. P. A. Martin (Chapel Hill, N. C., 1939), p. 220; Lawrence F. Hill (ed.), *Brazil* (Berkeley and Los Angeles, 1947), pp. 35-40 *passim*.
30. Henry W. Hilliard, *Politics and Pen Pictures* (New York, 1892), p. 367.
31. *Contribuições*, p. 325.
32. *Ibid.*, p. 560.

problems which faced the government caused his opponents to regard him as a skilful and crafty dictator.

The Conservatives had succeeded in nullifying the federalizing tendencies of the Ato Adicional through the use of the *poder moderador*, and during the period of his *de facto* rule Dom Pedro had continued this policy. The growth of liberal ideas, political changes in other countries, and the desire for constitutional government caused much of the party conflict to be centered upon the use of this power.[33]

Just a few years before the outbreak of the war with Paraguay, the progressive faction of the Liberal party had adopted a series of reforms aimed at decentralizing the government and bestowing upon the ministers of state the responsibility for the acts of the *poder moderador*, which hitherto had been an exclusive prerogative of the emperor.[34] Four years later, the Progressive Liberal party, whose break with the historical Liberals had widened, was in power, and propaganda for changes in the government increased.[35] Many of the ideas which had been prevalent in the House of Deputies in 1831 were revived. The Progressives demanded that the *poder moderador*, the council of state, and slavery be abolished, and that the national guard be curtailed. They also wanted education to be available to all and desired that the elections be free. Religious freedom, freedom of association, direct and general suffrage, separation of the police and the courts, a temporary Senate, election of the presidents of the provinces, and responsibility and independence of the magistrates were other reform measures demanded by this party.

As a means of propagandizing its ideas, the party founded the Club Radical in 1868 and held conferences to which the general public was freely admitted. The principal speakers at these conferences were such men as Godoye Vasconcellos, Liberato Barroso, Silveira da Matta, Rangel Pestana, and Gaspar da Silveira Martins. It is significant to note that these names were among the signatures on the Republican Manifesto in 1870.

On July 16, 1868, Dom Pedro by use of the *poder moderador* staged a coup d'état which removed the Liberals who enjoyed an almost complete majority in the House of Deputies; he called a Conservative to form a new ministry. Although the empire at that time was successfully passing through a critical period in its history, and the Emperor was at the zenith of his power, many Brazilian his-

33. Pereira da Silva, *Memórias do meu tempo*, I, 91, 92; *Contribuições*, pp. 542-549.
34. Calogeras, p. 233.
35. Rocha Pombo, *História do Brasil* (Rio de Janeiro, n.d.), X, 75.

torians regard this move as the beginning of the fall of the mon-archy.[36] The factors behind the coup d'état delineate the relation-ship which had existed between the Emperor and the parties before the war, and they indicate what was to follow during the later years of the empire.

When one considers that the Liberal party had been in power since 1862, and that during this time it had consolidated itself in the cities and the provinces of the empire, one realizes the far-reaching effect of the change of ministry upon the country. The president of the Liberal cabinet which fell was Zacarias de Goes e Vasconcellos, a man who was not exceptionally brilliant, but who was beloved by the members of his party. He was a politician who possessed great skill.[37] Nabuco de Araujo said of him: "the party was his spiritual family, he would have sacrificed his heart to it." He had few weak points and "his position reminded one of a ship of war, with its portholes closed, the decks cleared, crews at their posts, alone, un-boardable, prepared for action."[38]

Thus, a party man (*um homem de partido*) was the leader of the cabinet during the crucial period of the Paraguayan War when Dom Pedro called upon the Baron de Caxias to lead the Brazilian forces. The Liberal leader would have preferred a Liberal general for the office of commander in chief of the armies,[39] but in a situa-tion so serious the Emperor made the selection upon the basis of talent. His minister did not let the matter end there, but sought and found opportunities to discredit and annoy the old general.[40] Critics of Zacarias consider this as evidence of his lack of statesmanship and of his inability to consider anything beyond party interests. The resignation of the cabinet on July 16, 1868, had as pretext the refusal of the cabinet to accept the imperial selection of Salles Torres Homem as senator, but actually the fall was the result of the threat-ened resignation of the Baron de Caxias.[41]

The collapse of the Zacarias ministry, which had an almost unani-mous majority in the House of Deputies, and the appointment of the Conservative Itaborahi to form the new cabinet aroused indignation

36. *Contribuições*, p. 790; Tobias Monteiro, *Pesquisas e depoimentos para a história* (Rio de Janeiro, 1913), p. 117.
37. *Contribuições*, p. 791.
38. *Ibid.*
39. Pereira da Silva, *Memórias do meu tempo*, II, 70, 71.
40. *Ibid.*, II, 84.
41. Monteiro, *Pesquisas e depoimentos* . . . , pp. 116-117; Pereira da Silva, *Memórias do meu tempo*, II, 84, 89; *Contribuições*, p. 542.

in political circles of the empire. José Bonifácio, a member of the House of Deputies, proposed the following resolution, which was approved by the House:

The House of Deputies views with deep regard and general surprise the strange appearance of the present Cabinet, made of members from its group and symbolizing a new policy, wherein something other than a parliamentary question has caused the fall of its predecessors. Sincere friend of the parliamentary system and of the constitutional monarchy, the House regrets this singular factor, it has not nor can it have confidence in the Ministry.[42]

Whatever had been the motives of the Emperor, it is certain that from this time there was a marked change in the political beliefs of the influential people of Brazil. There appeared a double phenomenon, a progressive decline in the belief in constitutional monarchy and a progressive increase in aspiration for a new regime, a new order of things. Ottoni wrote that this phenomenon was caused by "the discredit which the imperial blow cast upon the institution and the natural evolution of the democratic ideas."[43]

Nabuco de Araujo, in criticizing the Emperor's use of the *poder moderador* to dismiss the Zacarias cabinet, said, "The *poder moderador* is able to call whom it wishes to organize a new ministry, that person holds an election and the election makes the majority in the House of Deputies. Such is the representative system in our country!"[44]

The dismissal of the cabinet seemed to arouse and inspire the Liberals. Newspapers throughout the country did not hesitate to brand the deed as despotic. Francisco Octaviano, Joaquim Manoel de Macedo, and others, who in 1868 directed the *Diário do Pôvo*, published an editorial in which they asserted that "the circumstances of the country are extremely grave. In foreign affairs there is a disastrous war and internally it presents a miserable spectacle." The editorial went on to assert:

for us there is only one capital interest. And this interest is nothing else save the stubborn effort which for years, either openly or secretely, the emperor has worked to destroy the legitimate parties, without whose action the representative system transforms itself into despotism. Things have reached the point where all decisions come from the top of the pyramid. It is the crown that governs.[45]

42. *Contribuições*, p. 794; *Jornal do Comercio* (Sept. 7, 1922), p. 341.
43. *Contribuições*, p. 794.
44. *Ibid.*
45. Rocha Pombo, X, 85, 86.

The *Constitutional,* a Pernambuco Conservative organ, complained:

the wicked policy of government by the emperor has created the desperate situation in which we find ourselves. . . . Such government is not of the Nation by the Nation, it is government of the emperor by the emperor. The Nation is divided and lacks unity to the proportion that the power is concentrated in the hands of one person only.[46]

During the same year the Liberal party split into two factions, the Historic Liberals and the Progressive Liberals. The *Reform,* organ of the Club da Reforma, published the Liberal manifesto in 1869. The manifesto demanded most of the reforms which the Liberal party had fostered since 1831, but its conclusion stated that these were only the ideas which the party considered most urgent at the moment.[47] The opening statement of the manifesto was a challenge to the empire, "Reform or revolution" (*Ou a reforma ou a revolução*).[48] Nabuco de Araujo, frightened at the radical stand taken by the party, wrote to a friend that "the cause of monarchy is declining because the Conservatives betray it and the Liberals do not defend it."[49]

The *poder moderador,* which was the focus of much of the Liberal complaint, was the fourth power of the Brazilian Constitution and was designed to harmonize the other three powers. This power was the key to the entire constitutional system and was incarnate in the person of the emperor himself.[50] Legally and morally, the emperor was forced to intervene in the affairs of the country. Either of the two parties, once having secured the control of the government, could and often did manipulate the elections so that it remained in power over a period of years. Only the use of the *poder moderador* permitted the opposition to win an election. When such a situation arose, the Emperor drew upon himself the hostility and imprecations of those whom he had forced from office. The ill-will of the "outs" was invariably turned upon Dom Pedro, and the "ins" were not particularly gratified when they were intrusted with the government.[51]

A noted Argentinian writer who visited the empire during this

46. *Contribuições,* p. 543.
47. Rocha Pombo, X, 77.
48. *Contribuições,* p. 543.
49. *Ibid.*
50. Calogeras, p. 220.
51. *Ibid.,* p. 221.

period remarked that "In Brazil there are parties without means of communication in the press, and there are newspapers without corresponding parties."[52] A more careful examination might have revealed to the Argentinian that those he saw as parties were not such, but were only men who associated in groups in order to obtain and exploit power. In most instances Liberals and Conservatives were mere humble creatures of the Emperor. Silveira Martins, after having been a minister, said that "The ministers do only that which the Emperor decides!"[53]

Immediately after the coronation of Dom Pedro a search for a bride for the young Emperor had been launched. On April 20, 1842, an agreement had been made for the marriage of the Emperor to Princess Thereza, sister of Ferdinand of the Two Sicilies. The marriage took place by proxy one year later, May 30, 1843, and the bride arrived in Rio de Janeiro on September 3, 1843. Two sons were born to the imperial couple, but both of them died in infancy; later two daughters, Isabel and Leopoldina, were born. Dom Pedro spent much of his free time with his daughters and he showed great concern for their education. Frequently he served as their instructor.

The Brazil of Dom Pedro in 1870 had an estimated population of 10,500,000.[54] Since the birth of the Emperor the population of the country had doubled itself. New forces had appeared in the economy of the country, and the capitalist and the worker were beginning to occupy important places in Brazilian civilization. The balance of power in the imperial government was shifting from the *fazendeiro* of the Northeast to the commercial and coffee barons of the South, the *paulista*. The man who was symbolic of this new class and of the economic position of Brazil in 1870 was Irineu Evangelista de Souza, Viscount of Mauá.[55] The period of the fifties and the sixties had been one of adjustment to the technological progress of the latter half of the nineteenth century. Mauá opened up the Amazon to commerce and introduced the use of the steamboat on that river.[56] He arranged for Rio Grande do Sul to have transatlantic communication, built ports, and became the first and greatest railroad builder in Brazil. He also built highways and telegraph lines, founded factories, and

52. Anfriso Fialho, *História da fundação da república no Brasil* (Rio de Janeiro, 1891), p. 21.
53. *Ibid.*, p. 23.
54. Normano, *Brazil, A Study of Economic Types*, p. 81.
55. *Ibid.*, p. 89.
56. *Papers Relating to the Foreign Relations of the United States* (Washington, D. C., 1870), p. 285 (letter from James R. Bond to Mr. Fish). Hereinafter cited as *Foreign Relations*.

introduced the use of gas lights in the city of Rio de Janeiro. He was referred to appropriately by one historian as "the Caxias of our economic unity."[57]

Brazil, which had lost her prominent position as an exporter of cotton after the invention of the cotton gin and the development of new techniques in the production of cotton cloth, had been able to regain her place in the export of that product during the years of the Civil War in the United States. This situation stimulated the production of cotton in the province of Ceará, which previously had only three times exceeded 500,000 pounds of output annually. During the year 1871-1872, Ceará produced 2,500,000 pounds of cotton. However, this production rate soon declined rapidly and at the time of the fall of the empire cotton was cultivated only in small plots.

Brazil's position in the coffee market was more advantageous. Her production had risen from 18.18 per cent of the world's production in the decade 1820-1829 to 49.09 per cent in the decade 1870-1879, and the increase was to continue throughout the nineteenth century.[58]

In 1870 Brazil's exports exceeded her imports by $150,400,000. During the preceding year the United States imported $25,000,000 worth of raw materials from Brazil, and the United States' minister at Rio de Janeiro complained that Brazil imported only $6,000,000 worth of material from the United States.[59] He said that Brazil used this surplus by "investing it in iron, cotton, and woolen goods, building her roads, cultivating her fields, and encouraging the manufactories of England, Belgium and Germany."[60]

Despite the waste caused by the Paraguayan War, the poor means of communication, the absence of capital, and the high rate of illiteracy, Brazil was entering an area of rapid economic expansion. Dom Pedro, cognizant of the situation, said in his Speech from the Throne of May 6, 1870, "the moral and material development of the Empire depends essentially upon the diffusion of knowledge to all classes of society, the improvement of communication, the encouragement of free labor, which is the principal source of our wealth."[61] During the 1870's efforts were made to remove the obstacles to economic progress. Immigration was encouraged and efforts were made to improve the country's school system. In 1878, night schools of agriculture were organized in some provinces. Much attention was

57. Normano, *Brazil, A Study of Economic Types*, p. 91.
58. *Ibid.*, p. 40.
59. *Ibid.*, p. 194.
60. *Foreign Relations*, p. 285.
61. *Contribuições*, p. 534.

given to the construction of railroads. Consequently, railway lines ✓ increased from 380 miles in 1870 to 650 miles in 1874 and to 1,354 ✓ miles in 1878.[62]

During the years before 1870 São Paulo had not been the economic equal of the northern provinces. However, in the period 1872-1877 the Paulista percentage of national exports rose to 11.41 per cent while the exports of Pernambuco fell to 8.94 per cent, whereas in the period 1862-1867 Paulista exports had been only 4.59 per cent of the national exports while those of Pernambuco had been 13.96 per cent.[63]

The city of Rio de Janeiro in 1870 had a population of about 500,-000. Dom Pedro's capital was about six miles in length, and, considering the area occupied by the city, it might have been assumed that Rio would have had a large population. Much of the space, however, was occupied by the beautiful gardens which were a part of many of the homes in the suburbs of the city. Not many decades before the city had had a reputation for being a filthy place, but much had been done to improve sanitary conditions. The streets were carefully paved with squared stones and the roads in the suburbs of the city were well macadamized. An excellent sewer system had been begun during the 1860's and its completion in the next decade removed another sore spot from the city.

One of the most important buildings in the city was the Hospital da Misericórdia, which a foreign visitor described as an "establishment conducted on a magnificent scale, under the direction of a committee of gentlemen, and zealously ministered to by the sisters of charity, whose Christian care of the inmates makes no distinction of sect or creed."[64]

The shops of the city were described as "neatly kept," and although small, they were furnished with every article of European luxury and utility. Magnificent statues were found in many of the squares of the city. The theater of São Pedro d'Alcantara was in the Largo do Rocio, and in a nearby square there was a fine equestrian statue of Dom Pedro I. This statue (which is the work of the French sculptor Louis Rochet, a student of David d'Angers) is regarded by many critics as one of the finest bronze statues in the world.[65]

One of the largest squares in the city was the Campo de Santa

62. *Ibid.*, p. 536.
63. *Ibid.*, p. 709.
64. William Scully, *Brazil, Its Provinces and Chief Cities* (London, 1866), pp. 152-153.
65. *Ibid.*, p. 155.

Anna. It contained no statues, but there was a fountain near its center where hundreds of slave women were accustomed to do their owners' laundry. On one side of this square was the Senate and on the other were the offices of the minister of war. The other two ends of the square were occupied by military barracks on one side and the Italian Opera House on the other.

There were more than forty-six primary schools for both sexes in the city. There were also a commercial school, naval and military colleges, and the College of Dom Pedro II. In addition to these institutions which were supported by the government, there were about twenty private schools.

One of Dom Pedro's favorite imperial palaces was located at São Christovão about three miles from Rio de Janeiro. The exterior of this palace was not imposing, but its interior was tastefully and suitably furnished and decorated. The grounds of the palace were a source of attraction. The fine avenues of trees, the lakes crossed by rustic bridges, and the beautifully arranged beds showing many specimens of the flora of the country were some of the chief attractions.

After Dom João VI brought the Portuguese court to Rio de Janeiro in 1808, that city became the social, political, and economic center of the country. It retained that position throughout the period of the empire. The *fazendeiro* was drawn to the court not because of the new economic possibilities, but because "the splendor and luxury of the court attracted the Brazilian agrarian aristocracy. The *fazendeiro*, a monarch of his own *fazenda*, the possessor of *de facto* unlimited power at home, came to the capital to greet the official monarch of the country and to live in the sun of his splendor."[66] The appearance of the capitalist, the industrialist, and the free worker had signaled the end of rule by this class. Therefore, those who made Rio their home in 1870 were turning to politics to mend their fortunes and were becoming confirmed inhabitants of the city.

Brazil in 1870 contained many able men who demanded change, and the desire for reform could not be suppressed. The aroused Liberal dissatisfaction had mounted during the last two years of the war with Paraguay. The Liberal manifesto of May, 1869, stated that the mission of the Liberal party in Brazil was to realize and to develop the democratic element of the Constitution and to secure the greatest amplification and guarantee of individual and political lib-

66. Normano, *Brazil, A Study of Economic Types*, p. 71.

erty.[67] The program which was outlined in this manifesto was virtually a demand for the creation of a republic.

It may be noted that when Brazil had declared herself independent of Portugal in 1822, the idea of establishing a republic had been firmly intrenched in the minds of many of her most able statesmen. They looked upon the monarchy in Brazil as a temporary expedient, a form of government which would be quickly replaced by a republic.[68] José Bonifácio, a firm and sincere believer in the monarchy and a skilled politician as well, was able to make the monarchy permanent, but this was not done without opposition from the proponents of the republican idea. This can be seen in the turbulence of the government between 1822 and 1848. It was only the personal influence of Dom Pedro II which secured peace for the country after 1848. During 1863 the American minister, James W. Webb, wrote to the United States secretary of state concerning the future of the monarchy: Dom Pedro II "will be the last Emperor, and Brazil will become a Republic—and this, too, without a struggle." The minister then remarked that because of the growth of liberal and democratic principles "the best people in Brazil calmly look forward to the day, when, by a slight change in their Constitution, the Empire will noiselessly glide into a Republic."[69]

It was only a short step from the Liberal manifesto to the organization of a Republican party. During November, 1870, a number of leaders of the radical faction of the Liberal party met and considered raising the banner of the Republican party. On December 3, 1870, the party was organized, and on that date, in the city of Rio de Janeiro, the first issue of the organ of the party, *A República*, containing the celebrated *Manifesto Republicano*, was published.

The manifesto appealed to the people of Brazil and asserted that the people alone could refute the program which it outlined. It stated that "in the regime of oppression and violence, to conspire is our right," and it added that it was the duty of the party to discuss the deceit and corruption of the government.[70] The signers of the manifesto pointed out that the old political parties had been reduced to impotency; hence, demands for reform could not be pleaded on constitutional grounds. They insisted that the system of privilege in all of its relations with society be ended. All arbitrary distinctions,

67. *Jornal do Comercio* (Sept. 7, 1922), p. 341.
68. *Contribuições*, p. 549; Charles W. Turner, *Ruy Barbosa* (New York, 1945), p. 94.
69. Williams, p. 289.
70. Rocha Pombo, X, 77.

such as privilege of race, of learning, of position, of religion, and all distinctions "which create in the heart of civil and political society the monstrous superiority of one above all or of the few above the many" were denounced.[71] The moral decay of the country, its lack of administrative organization, and the economic troubles which assailed it were regarded as results of monarchial ineptness.

The manifesto was published in many cities of the empire. In Minas and São Paulo it aroused great enthusiasm, and in many localities Republican clubs and journals were founded, especially in São Paulo where a regular Republican party was organized. The assumption of the program of the Liberal party by the Conservatives and the general inability to distinguish the platforms of the two parties led Tavares Bastos on December 23, 1871, to declare that the Republican party was coming to be the only party of the opposition.[72]

The appearance of a republican party in Brazil in 1870 did not arouse fears in imperial circles; the Emperor, when informed of the manifesto and urged not to permit men of republican ideas to hold office, replied: "If the Brazilians do not want me as their Emperor, I shall become a professor."[73] Although weak at first, during the coming twenty years imperial policies and the growth of progressive ideas were to cause powerful adherents to gather around the Republican banner.

A problem of more immediate importance confronting the statesmen of the empire in 1870 was that of emancipation of the Brazilian slaves. Despite the dangers inherent in any attempted solution of this problem, Liberal demands that it be considered by the Parliament continued. The law of September 7, 1831, had declared that all slaves brought into Brazil from other countries, except those who were employed on ships from countries where slavery was still permitted, were free. On September 4, 1850, the bill sponsored by Eusebio de Queiroz had definitely ended the slave trade at its source; that is, no more slaves were permitted to enter the country. This measure indicated that slavery in Brazil was doomed. There remained another step by which the extinction of slavery could be hastened, a method which had been used in the Republic of Argentina on February 2, 1813, in New Granada on July 7, 1821, and in Portugal on July 24, 1856. This step was to make free all children born of slave mothers.[74]

After 1850 several projects in support of this method had been proposed, but Zacarias de Goes e Vasconcellos first raised the question

71. *Ibid.*, X, 79.
72. *Contribuições*, p. 545.
73. *Ibid.*, p. 557.
74. *Ibid.*, p. 405.

in Parliament in 1867, when reference in the Speech from the Throne was made to giving consideration to the slavery issue in such a way that the country's principal industry, agriculture, would not be injured. During the same year the government named a commission composed of Nabuco de Araujo, Salles Torres Homem, and Sousa Franco, with the Viscount de São Vicente as secretary, to study the problem and to seek a solution which would be satisfactory to all.

The Speech from the Throne of 1868 mentioned that the problem was being considered by a commission, but in 1869 and in 1870 no reference was made to emancipation. However, the Viscount de São Vicente included the request that some effort be made for reform of the servile element in the program of his ministry. In the House of Deputies several proposals concerning gradual emancipation were made.[75] In response to the Speech from the Throne of 1870, the House declared: "The House of Deputies is convinced that reform legislation concerning the servile state cannot continue to be an indefinite and uncertain national aspiration."[76] The following year, after the fall of São Vicente's ministry, the Viscount de Rio Branco became president of the ministry. The Speech from the Throne of May 3, 1871, asked that consideration of the problem be delayed no longer.

During the long session of the legislature, Rio Branco, who bore the brunt of the attack against the proposed gradual emancipation bill, made forty-one speeches, of which twenty-one dealt with defense of the servile reform bill.[77] The measure was finally approved by the Senate on September 28, 1871. The law declared that children born of slave mothers were free. The owner could receive an indemnity of six hundred *milreis* and the child would remain in the care of his mother until eight years of age, at which time he would become a ward of the state, or the owner could retain the child until he was twenty-one, at which time he would be freed without indemnification. Thus, it seemed that one problem which confronted the empire in 1870 had been satisfactorily solved. But it was soon proved that only complete and immediate abolition of slavery would satisfy the opponents of that institution. After a few years of quiet the opponents of slavery were to rise again with a demand this time for complete and immediate abolition.

In 1870 the religious question, which was to contribute to the causes which led to the fall of Dom Pedro II, had not developed into

75. *Ibid.*, p. 408.
76. *Ibid.*
77. Percy A. Martin, "Slavery and Abolition in Brazil," *The Hispanic American Historical Review*, XIII, 177.

an open contest between church and state. However the factors which were to make the question a national and international issue had been present for almost a decade. These factors had operated both upon the Emperor and upon the Brazilian clergy. Dom Pedro, as a Catholic sovereign, marched in regular religious processions, attended Mass, and performed dutifully all of the tasks of a pious monarch, yet he was not a fervent Catholic and regarded religion as an essentially personal matter. He was friendly to Protestants and early in his reign began an acquaintance with Alexandre Herculano, a Portuguese proponent of reform within the Catholic church. During his trips abroad he did not hesitate to visit Protestant churches and Jewish synagogues. During his visit to Utah he listened to a sermon by a Morman minister. His lack of fervor led many of his countrymen to consider him a freethinker and even an atheist. Those who believed this were in error, although the Emperor was certainly not an orthodox Roman Catholic. Perhaps Joaquim Nabuco, who referred to him as a "limited Catholic," best described his religious beliefs.[78] In addition to his limited Catholicism, the Emperor, before the advent of the religious question, had served as grand master of the Masons, around whom the religious issue revolved.

Freemasonry had existed in Brazil before 1822, and up to 1864 there had been no hostility between lodge and church. Masons were members of the *irmandades* (brotherhoods consisting of laymen connected with the church), and during the period just before the beginning of the conflict many members of the clergy were members of the lodges. In 1864 Pope Pius IX condemned Masonry in his encyclical *Quanta Cura*, but Dom Pedro, cognizant of the peaceful relations which had existed in Brazil between Masonry and the church and of the difficulties which the encyclical could create in his country, refused approval of its circulation in Brazil. Officially the clergy of Brazil knew nothing of the encyclical, yet many of them began to obey the papal order to withdraw from Masonic organizations. Thus, in 1870 Brazil's government and the church were seemingly at peace, but under the surface sides were being taken and tension was mounting. The contest which followed was to deprive the empire of one of its strongest supporters.

Dom Pedro's Brazil in 1870 was a country which was united and whose government had been stabilized by the careful policies of her able Emperor. Victorious in the costly war with Paraguay, the empire had acquired new prestige in the eyes of the world.

78. *Ibid.*

Chapter Two

The Military Class at the Conclusion of the Paraguayan War

The war with Paraguay had found Brazil very poorly prepared. There had been ample warning that a conflict was imminent, but the government seemed indifferent to the danger and took no strenuous measures of preparation. In the conflict against Rosas, the Argentine dictator, and Oribe, a former leader of the Uruguayan Blanco, a conservative political party, Brazil at least had had Caxias, with an army of 20,000 men in Rio Grande do Sul. But in the conflict of 1865-1870 only the invasion of Mato Grosso stimulated Brazil to intense activity.[1]

At the time of the invasion Brazil had less than 17,000 men in the armed forces. The only unit readily available to oppose the Paraguayans was the small army under General Menna Barreto, which, weakened by the campaign it had just completed against the Blancos of Uruguay and lacking suitable equipment and uniforms, was in no position to offer effective opposition to the invaders. Brazil's remaining troops were stationed in different provinces.[2]

After the invasion of Mato Grosso steps were immediately taken to increase the strength of the army. Late in the year 1865 its strength had risen to 35,698 officers and men. Included in this number were four lieutenant generals, eight field marshals, and sixteen brigadier generals. There were 120 officers of the Engineer Corps, 79 on the *Estado maior*, first class,[3] and 109 on the *Estado mairo*, second class. There were also 196 officers of the hospital corps and 38 chaplains. The total strength of the artillery was 3,376, including a battalion of

1. Souza Docea, *Causas da Guerra com o Paraguay* (Porto Alegre, 1919), p. 100; Octaviano Pereira de Sousa, ''Historia da guerra do Paraguay,'' *RIHGB,* CLVI, 62.
2. Docea, p. 101.
3. Sousa, p. 62.

engineers. There were 2,103 cavalrymen and 11,162 *Voluntários da patria*, 14,805 national guardsmen, 16 student officers, and more than 380 servants (*agregados*).[4]

A law passed by the Parliament in 1866 raised the strength of the army to 60,000 men. The distinction between garrison and movable corps having been ended during 1865, the former garrison or fixed corps—that is, corps which were not to be transferred beyond their home province—were organized into twenty-two light infantry battalions. The tables of organization for these battalions were similar to those for the light infantry battalions of the regular army. There was an *Estado maior*, consisting of one lieutenant colonel, one major, one adjutant, one quartermaster, and one secretary. The battalion *Estado menor* consisted of the non-commissioned officers of the battalion headquarters. These were one sergeant-adjutant, one quartermaster sergeant, one armorer, one gunstock maker, one chief trumpeter, one master of music, and twelve musicians.[5]

The infantry battalion, in many instances, consisted of the *Estados maior* and *menor* and one company. The company contained one captain, one lieutenant, one second lieutenant, one first sergeant, two second sergeants, one quartermaster sergeant, six squad leaders, six corporals, 658 *soldados*, and two drummers. The total strength of the infantry battalion was 679 men. The Brazilian artillery was raised to five battalions, in addition to the horse artillery. This was in conformity with the plan which had been devised in 1851 for raising the strength of this service. Artillery battalions usually contained 617 officers and men. Before the invasion of Paraguay the cavalry had been reduced to three corps. It was reinforced by the addition of five corps of light cavalry. Their table of organization was similar to that of the infantry except that the ranking officer could be a colonel or a lieutenant colonel. Other differences were the addition of a veterinarian and a riding master to the *Estado maior*. A saddle maker and a blacksmith were included among the enlisted officers. The corps and companies of *artifices*, which had existed prior to 1865, were replaced by companies of *operários*, who established themselves in the arsenals and manufactured powder and explosives under the supervision of the minister of war.

In October, 1867, Brazil had 42,873 men in the army. These men were in the following units:[6]

4. *Ibid.*
5. *Ibid.*, p. 63.
6. *Ibid.*, p. 272.

Special Corps	146
First Artillery Corps	717
First Cavalry Corps	2,908
First Infantry Corps	10,934
Second Artillery Corps	2,108
Second Cavalry Corps	2,991
Second Infantry Corps	9,653
Third Artillery Corps	248
Third Cavalry Corps	3,589
Third Infantry Corps	8,015
Battalion of Engineers	701
Transportation Corps	863
Total	42,873
Sick	10,708
Effectives	32,165

The army of 6,000 veterans which had recently concluded the campaign in the Montevideo area served as the nucleus for the formation of Brazil's army of volunteers. This army consisted of two divisions: the first commanded by Manuel Luiz Osorio, at that time a brigadier general, and the second under Brigadier General José Luiz Menna Barreto, Brazil's great cavalry leader. The majority of these troops were volunteers from the southern provinces of Brazil. Since they had volunteered at the same time that Brazil sent her troops into Uruguay, there had been little opportunity for them to be trained and disciplined. Their equipment was insufficient and, lacking proper uniforms, they presented a colorful but motley appearance. This was also true of the troops who came to join the southern army after the invasion by López, whether they came from Rio de Janeiro or from the northern provinces.

The initial concentration of troops was in Uruguay; later the camp was moved to the city of Concordia in the Argentine province of Entre-Rios. Here because of the intense cold of that region and the quality of the food, which in most instances was beef, many of the recruits who arrived from Brazil's northern provinces were frequent victims of illness. Poor sanitary conditions caused many of them to suffer dysentery.

Many of the troops who came to the south to take up arms in defense of their country were tough men from the backlands of northern Brazil, or sertões. Bahia sent thirteen battalions of Voluntários da pátria, among whom were men of this type. These men were strong, although at first glance they did not appear so. "Many of them were ugly, stooped-shoulders and ungainly, their *normally down trodden being* was aggravated by a dour look which gave them an air of depressing humility."[7] This seeming listlessness could be transformed instantly; "he [the soldier] straitens up, becomes a new man, with new lines in his posture and bearing; his head held high now, above his massive shoulders; his gaze straightforward and unflinching."[8] Such a person, who reached manhood "without ever having been a child," regarded life itself as a conflict without truce and became strong, expert, resigned, and practical. The backlanders, inured to suffering and hardship, strong, tenacious, and vigorous, did excellent service for their country during the Paraguayan War.

In contrast with the *sertanejo* of the backlands of the north was the cowboy of the southern plains, the *gaúcho*. The latter, finding his environment more friendly, had a more chivalrous and attractive bearing. He was jovial, valiant, eloquent of speech, and swaggering. Compared to that of the *sertanejo*, his clothing was like the garb of a circus performer. In the annals of the Rio de la Plata republics his daring and courage are legendary:

To the shrill and vibrant sound of trumpets, he will gallop across the pampas, the butt of his lance firmly couched in his stirrup; like a madman, he will plunge into the thick of the fight; with a shout of triumph, he is swallowed up from sight in the swirl of combat, where nothing is to be seen but the flashing of sword on sword; transforming his horse into a projectile, he will rout squadrons and trample his adversaries, or—he will fall in the struggle which he entered with so supreme a disregard for his life.[9]

The *sertanejo* was less theatrically heroic, but he was stronger and possessed a more enduring bravery.

Brazil availed itself of all sources of manpower. The cities and *fazendas* provided soldiers for the armies, and opportunity was afforded slaves to enlist in the army. The 20,000 slaves who served in the war were promised that they and their families would be freed, but this promise was not kept in all cases.

The initial concentration of the troops in Concordia seemingly afforded ample opportunity for the training of the recruits. Because of the absence of foresight and planning, little or no advantage was taken of this opportunity. An eyewitness testified that during the four months between the conquest of Montevideo and the passage of the Parana River, there was no firing practice in any of the units.[10]

7. Euclides da Cunha, *Rebellion in the Backlands*, trans. Samuel Putnam (Chicago, 1944), p. 89.
8. *Ibid.*, p. 90.
9. *Ibid.*, p. 94.
10. Sousa, p. 67.

The Brazilian forces, still in the process of being organized, were inferior to the Paraguayan soldiers. But their arms were superior to those of the enemy and with the aid of intrepid fighters, as were the *gaúchos* and *sertanejos*, the Brazilian infantry was soon in condition to meet the foe advantageously.

The officers who led the imperial armies were not the best, but there were leaders of merit among them. The army itself had a tradition of bravery, self-denial, and patriotism. It cannot be denied that the war was poorly directed in the first years, and that it was needlessly prolonged.[11] Yet the great blunders and errors which prolonged the war were not due to the poor quality of Brazilian officers and soldiers, but to the extreme prudence which characterized the high command at the beginning. Brazilian historians are not reluctant to give another cause for the length of the war. One wrote that the Treaty of the Triple Alliance was an excellent political move, but that it had one vulnerable point, for it placed the supreme command of the war in the hands of the Argentine President, Mitre.[12]

Brazil's great heroes of the Paraguayan War were Luiz Alves de Lima e Silva, Marquês and afterward Duke of Caxias, "The Chief Patron of the Army"; and Manuel Luiz Osorio, "The Lance of the Empire." Caxias, Brazil's greatest general, was born in Rio de Janeiro in 1803; Osorio was born in 1809 in Rio Grande do Sul. Caxias was descended from a long line of military men, and early in life he displayed an interest in military affairs. He offered his services to his country when he was fourteen years of age, and within a year he was a second lieutenant. At the Military School in Rio de Janeiro he made a brilliant record as a student of military engineering. At the age of twenty-one, holding the rank of lieutenant, he was appointed adjutant of the Battalion of the Emperor. He marched with that battalion to oppose the Portuguese forces in Bahia during the war for independence.[13] On that memorable April 7, 1831, when Dom Pedro I abdicated, Caxias organized a battalion of officers whose mission it was to police the city of Rio de Janeiro until the provisional government could be established to maintain order. After the establishment of the new government he was given the responsibility for organizing the Municipal Guards.

In 1839 he was named governor of the province of Maranhão and

11. *Ibid.*
12. *Ibid.*, p. 497; Viscount de Ouro Preto, *A marinha d'outrora* (Rio de Janeiro, 1894), "Tractado da Triplice Allianca," Annex, p. 4, Article Three.
13. Lima Figueiredo, *Grandes soldados do Brasil* (2nd ed.; Rio de Janeiro, 1942), pp. 13, 61.

became the commander of the troops which operated against the rebel forces there. One year after his arrival, order was restored. Caxias was then elected to the House of Deputies as the representative from the province of Maranhão. Upon his arrival at Rio de Janeiro he was made Baron de Caxias and was sent to pacify the provinces of São Paulo and Minas Gerais. This mission accomplished, he was sent to Rio Grande do Sul, where in 1845 he ended the revolution of the *farrapos*. This revolt was called the war of the *farrapos* because the gaúcho with his fringed breeches played a prominent role in the revolution.

After leading the Brazilian troops to victory over Rosas on February 2, 1852, at Monte Caseros, Caxias was named minister of war in 1855. In 1862 he was president of the council and minister of war. When the conflict with Paraguay began he proposed that the war be carried to the heart of that republic at once. Since the Liberals were in power, Caxias, a Conservative, was not immediately given the command of the armies. Only after two years of reverses was he placed in command of the Brazilian troops.[14] The departure of President Mitre of Argentina from the battle area permitted Caxias to demonstrate his ability as a general, and this he did to the satisfaction of all observers. Charles A. Washburn, an American diplomat who visited the Brazilian camp, described Caxias to López in the following manner: "I told him [López] that he [Caxias] was an old man who appeared to be very active and an excellent disciplinarian; that the allied camp was in a much better condition than I had ever seen it before, though I had visited it several times."[15] This general, who was admired by all of his troops and whose courageous and intelligent strategy led his forces to so many victories during the war, knew how to inspire the men under his command. He spoke truthfully when he told the Brazilian army just before the Battle of Avai that "the general and friend who this day leads you has never been defeated."[16]

Manuel Luiz Osorio, brave and impetuous, a beloved and skilful leader of troops, had a career similar to that of Caxias. He was straightforward in manner, and his honesty and strict adherence to principles made him generally respected. He was selected to command the Brazilian forces at the beginning of the war and distin-

14. "Luiz Alves de Lima e Silva, Duque de Caxias," *Encyclopedia e Dicionario Internacional*, IV (Rio de Janeiro, 1936).
15. Charles A. Washburn, *The History of Paraguay* (Boston, 1871), II, 187.
16. Figueiredo, p. 17.

guished himself at Itapiru, Passo da Patria, Estero Bellaco, and Tuyuti.

Osorio, a valiant old soldier, was a master of sarcasm, of which Dom Pedro himself was the victim on one occasion. While he was minister in the Sinimbu cabinet, at a very dull cabinet meeting Dom Pedro fell asleep. Osorio, observing this, raised his sword and let it fall to the floor with a loud crash. Dom Pedro, startled, asked: "General, did you let your sword fall like that during the war?" Osorio smiled and answered, "No, Majesty, I never slept in Paraguay."[17]

The Paraguayan forces which the Brazilian, Argentine, and Uruguayan armies opposed as early as November, 1864, numbered 80,000 trained and equipped troops. López, in answer to the appeal of Atanasio C. Aguirre, the leader of the Blanco party (the Uruguayan conservative party), had moved a portion of his troops across the Argentine provinces of Corrientes and Entre Rios in order to attack the Brazilians who were laying siege to the Blanco troops in Montevideo. This violation of Argentine territory brought Argentina into the war, and a treaty was signed between Brazil, Argentina, and the Colorados, the traditional liberal party of Uruguay's government. The Paraguayan invasion of defenseless Mato Grosso served no end that was beneficial to López. It divided Paraguay's forces and served to arouse Brazilian patriotism. The troops who had invaded the Argentine provinces captured Corrientes, but they were defeated at the Battle of Yatay, August 17, 1865, and another section of the invading army which had captured the Brazilian town of Uruguayana was forced to surrender the town on September 18, 1865. During the same year the Brazilian fleet, under the command of Admiral Barroso, destroyed the major units of Paraguay's fleet, and the naval part of the war became confined to the efforts of the Brazilian fleet to reduce the forts on the Paraguay River. These forts guarded the approaches to Asuncion.

Brazil and its allies, being unprepared for war, were forced to fight defensively during the first years of the conflict.[18] This was followed by the offensive campaign during which the Paraguayan armies were defeated and driven back into the interior, beyond Asunción, and during which López was killed by a Brazilian enlisted man. Caxias had returned to Rio de Janeiro with the statement that

17. *Ibid.*, p. 65.
18. Ouro Preto, *A marinha d'outrora*, pp. 37-40.

he was not a "Captain of the woods."[19] This was a reference to the fact that López, having lost almost all of his troops, had fled into the interior with about one hundred men. Caxias did not care to track him down. Consequently, the Count d'Eu was given command of the Brazilian forces in 1869. López was able to continue organized and guerrilla warfare until 1870.

The Count d'Eu, husband of Princess Isabel, had an excellent opportunity to win the hearts of the military during this last phase of the war. The young man, in the opinion of many, conducted the campaign in an excellent manner and was regarded as a great strategist.[20] But it was observed that he possessed little ability in gaining the approval and admiration of the military. He accorded small courtesy to officers of inferior rank, and many of the junior officers with whom he came in contact disliked him. Had he possessed the ability to be gracious and to make friends, he could have been one of their idols, as were Caxias, Osorio, Porto Alegre, Camara, Deodoro, Floriano, and many others.[21]

The victorious army, whose troops began returning to the cities, *fazendas*, and *sertões* of Brazil in 1870, had experienced a great revival of spirit. Not since 1831 had the military been called upon to play such an important part in the affairs of the nation. The victory did not affect only the army; it gave to all Brazilians a sense of pride and aroused their patriotism. Throughout the provinces of Brazil the returning troops were welcomed as heroes. Not only the great military leaders, but all of the army, the national guard, and especially the *Voluntários da pátria*, were received with magnificent celebrations. The legislative houses passed motions of congratulation, and enthusiasm reached the point where it was proposed that a statue of the Emperor be erected in a square in Rio de Janeiro. The proposal was not carried out, however, because Dom Pedro requested that the money raised for such a purpose be used in a more beneficial way for founding a school.[22]

There was a discordant note in the welcome accorded to some of the returning regiments. The government of the province of Rio de Janeiro seemed particularly concerned about the $200,000,000 cost of the war and the rise of military fervor in that province, and this concern was especially noted in the return of the *Voluntários da*

19. Lima, *O império brasileiro*, p. 145; José Wanderley de Araujo Pinho, "Pedro II e Cotegipe," *RIHGB*, CLII, 487.
20. Calogeras, p. 217.
21. Ernesto Mattoso, *Causas do meu tempo* (Bordeaux, 1916), p. 146.
22. Rocha Pombo, X, 342.

pátria. These units were dispersed quietly, without ceremony; their standards were put away and the bands were silent.[23] The Count d'Eu, the commander of these units, looked upon this as a "betrayal of his companions in arms," and he vigorously protested this action.[24]

A document published by the government stated that 83,000 men had been sent to Paraguay, and of that number about 24,000 had been killed in combat and numerous others had been wounded by enemy action.[25] Five thousand troops had been left in Paraguay as a garrison force. During the years that followed the war with Paraguay, the politicians who controlled Brazil deliberately neglected the army. While these *políticos* engaged in vocal exchanges, one contemporary observed:

A forgotten army existed in Brazil. This army was badly organized, poorly instructed and poorly paid; it was an army where there was one officer for thirteen soldiers; where the number of officers and the long period of peace made promotions difficult to obtain; where the poor soldier lived outside of regimental life, attached in small garrisons of twenty, ten, five and even two men in the towns of the interior. A situation which was unfavorable to the maintenence of discipline and was destructive in every respect.[26]

Despite the tendency for the parties to pay court to the heroes of the war, the tension between the military and the civilian leaders increased. "Little by little, this thought was growing in the minds of the military: the *políticos* are the enemies of the military."[27] The feeling of contempt for the *político* and of superiority over all civilians which had appeared during the war was now bolstered by resentment and hatred. Had it not been the soldier who had won the war of independence, who had fought and suffered for the creation of national unity, and who had saved the country in the war against Paraguay?[28] Having saved the country on former occasions, the military not surprisingly began to think that "they were predestined to be the saviors of Brazil from the odious machinations of party leaders and politicians."[29]

Victorious in two foreign campaigns, having defeated Rosas in 1852, and vanquished Paraguay after a long and difficult campaign

23. Pereira da Silva, *Memórias do meu tempo*, II, 118.
24. Lima, *O império brasileiro*, p. 146.
25. Pereira da Silva, *Memórias do meu tempo*, p. 118.
26. Galanti, V, 96-97.
27. Galanti, V, 96; Counselor Carlos Honario Benedicto Ottoni, *O advento da república no Brasil* (Rio de Janeiro, 1890), p. 82.
28. Calogeras, p. 261.
29. *Ibid.*, p. 262.

in 1865-1870, the army had just cause to be proud. However, it was observed that these accomplishments "increased [the army's] conceit and opinion of its importance without instilling in it a sense of discipline."[30] The soldiers of the ranks, and anyone who had been with the army, considered it a great honor to have been in Paraguay. The families of those who had distinguished themselves in Paraguay became a class set apart, above the ordinary Brazilians. They became members of a military nobility.[31]

During January, 1874, the Military College was separated from the Central College by the establishment of the Polytechnical College. Thus, the youths who were destined to become officers of the army were separated from their companions who were being trained for careers in civilian life. The change was designed to facilitate improvement in the education of the young officers, but it served only as a means of isolating the military students and making available to them a course of study which easily permitted the introduction of non-military subjects.[32] The students of the Military School became little concerned with the problems of war. Their school became a place for the training of philosophers and *políticos*. The positivist philosophy of Auguste Comte infiltrated the ranks of the students and even the ranks of the staff officers of the army. The military school also became a stronghold of the abolitionists, and their influence upon the military was evident in 1883 when the first postwar contest between the military and civilian politicians occurred.

The interest in politics which appeared among the student officers was matched by that of the returned army officers who, influenced by contact with their Republican brothers in arms from the Rio de la Plata, now had a desire for political power. This desire in officers of the highest ranks had long been satisfied by those who controlled the government. Officers of this rank, victorious in the war, now brought a new element into the politics of the empire. In the words of Rocha Pombo, "They passed from the fields of battle to the councils of the crown, which seemed to value them as an indispensable reinforcement to the weak, almost artificial vitality of that institution."[33] Officers of lesser rank, now aware of their importance, demanded that they too be permitted to play a major part in the politics of the country. One writer has described their political desires as an illness, and in his

30. Lima, *O império brasileiro*, p. 145.
31. Rocha Pombo, X, 342.
32. General Bibiano Sergio Macado da Fontoura Castallat, "Exercito," *Livro do Centenario, 1500-1900* (Rio de Janeiro, 1901), II, 24.
33. Rocha Pombo, X, 343.

opinion the army was "the victim of *Virus político* from which the military institutions of South America have suffered so much."[34]

It cannot be denied that contact with the Republicans of the Rio de la Plata influenced the Brazilian military.[35] The virus which infected them had been contacted from caudillos of the Plata region such as Rosas, Rivera, and López. The prestige and influence of these men in their own countries aroused the interest and envy of one Brazilian military officer in particular, a major destined to become the second president of the United States of Brazil: Floriano Peixoto. In a letter to a friend he praised López and said: "Such a man as that is what we need in Brazil."[36]

Admiration for the dictators of the Rio de la Plata did not direct the resentment of the officers toward Dom Pedro, even though the Emperor in all his long reign never indicated that he understood his generals. He was preoccupied with civil administration, as well as the arts and sciences, and devoted little time to the development of the army. The care and attention which European monarchs of his time gave to their armed forces was expended by Dom Pedro for the cultural, social, and economic improvement of his country. This attitude was tolerated by the officers because of their respect for the throne, and they directed their complaints to the civilian administrators of imperial policy.

In addition to their admiration for the dictators of the Plata region, Brazil's officers in some instances found themselves placed on the defensive because of the existence of slavery in Brazil.[37] Brazil at that time was not only unique in that it had a monarchial government, but also in that it retained this hated institution. That there was far more liberty in the empire of Brazil than in the "republics" of South America did not influence the citizens of other South American countries. To them a monarchy limited the freedom and liberty of its citizens, and they regarded Brazil's government as an interloper on a free continent. These factors, as well as a difference in race, had caused most of the other South American countries to sympathize with López in the conflict against Brazil. After the war, when all of the Brazilian parties, Conservative, Liberal, and Republican, sought to wed themselves to the victorious army, the same factors played a part in the army's selection of the Republican party for its mate in 1889.

34. Lima, *O império brasileiro*, p. 145.
35. *Ibid.*, p. 147.
36. *Ibid.*, p. 155.
37. Williams, p. 269.

The military gained some things more tangible than political theories from the contact with their Republican allies. Certain modes of dress passed over from the Republicans to the imperial troops: the hat worn on the side of the head, the whip secured to the wrist by a piece of silver, the wearing of silken trousers, and hair cut short and heavily oiled.[38] It was not until the last year of the monarchy that these evidences of arrogance and vanity began to disappear from the Brazilian armed forces.

The strongest bulwark devised by the monarchy against military interferences in the politics of the country was the selection of respected, high-ranking officers for prominent governmental positions. After the war the occupancy of certain high posts by military men became so commonplace that when such positions were not filled by generals the military became resentful.

The fall of the Zacarias cabinet in 1868 had signaled the entry of the military class into politics. During the years after the Paraguayan War the Conservatives cultivated the prestige of Caxias, who was to become their military champion, and the Liberals groomed Osorio as a military defender of their party. After the deaths of Caxias and Osorio, the Viscount de Pelotas was selected by the Liberals as their military chief, and Cotegipe, the most outstanding leader of the Conservatives, began to rouse the ambitions of Deodoro so that in the future he would become "our Caxias." That is, Deodoro as the Conservative military leader would be favored with high office, rising to the Senate, to the presidency of the Council of State, to the Ministry of War, and perhaps to the day when "the valiant sword will have its hilt decorated with the arms of nobility."[39]

However, the appearance of these soldiers in politics resulted in the widening of the gulf of misunderstanding between the civilian and military leaders. The qualities which had made these men effective leaders of troops in battle had little to do with their ability to play a brilliant part in the politics of the country.[40]

The flattery of men of greatest prestige in the army was only one phase of the *político*'s exploitation of the armed forces after 1870. During this period the army was the only class in the country which possessed an obvious *esprit de corps*, and the officers were the only group with a professional sense of honor. This feeling of class dis-

38. Fleiuss, *História administrativa* . . . , p. 411; Monteiro, *Pesquisas e depoimentos* . . . , p. 146.

39. Rocha Pombo, X, 6.

40. Pedro Calmon, *História social do Brasil* (2nd ed.; São Paulo, 1933), II, 252.

tinction had been intensified after the war, and at the same time it was supported by a sense of superiority. The military, having endured the hardships of the war, felt themselves purified by the grandeur and heroism of a task well done, and all of this gave them an arrogant conviction of their superiority to civilians. They looked upon the non-military man as effeminate and weak. Their superiority stemmed from their self-denial, morality, and the austere simplicity and poverty of their life.

In many respects their attitude toward the political condition of the country, and toward the civilian element which controlled it, was correct. Before the *político* came to him, the military man had not been ambitious. He was frugal, poor, and honest. After the infiltration of the *político* into his ranks, the military man was no longer without ambition, and much of his poverty vanished; only the sense of professional honor remained. The failure of the military men who entered the political arena to understand the absence of a sense of professional honor among the *políticos* was to become another source of the "military questions" whose appearance signaled the decline of the monarchy.[41]

41. Olivira Vianna, "A queda do império," *Contribuições*, p. 845.

Chapter Three

Marshal Manoel Deodoro da Fonseca and the First Phase of the Military Question

Manoel Deodoro da Fonseca was born on August 5, 1827, in the city of Alagoas, provincial capital of the province of the same name. His father was Lieutenant Colonel Manoel Mendes da Fonseca and his mother was Rosa Maria Paulina da Fonseca. Both of the parents were natives of the province of Alagoas. It is possible that some members of the Fonseca family had been residents of Brazil since the time of the Dutch occupation in the north.[1] In 1831, the year of the abdication of Dom Pedro I, Deodoro's father was commandant of the military in the province of Alagoas. During the last days of the reign of the first emperor he was promoted to lieutenant colonel and commanded the Sixteenth Infantry Battalion.[2] For a few years following the abdication of Dom Pedro I, Manoel Mendes da Fonseca, who was suspected of remaining loyal to the former emperor, was deprived of his military rank by the government. In 1836, having regained the confidence of the government, he commanded the troops of the province when the rebellion of the Cabanas of Pernambuco was suppressed. Three years later, in addition to commanding the military of Alagoas Province, he was a member of the provincial council and judge of the provincial court.[3]

The career of this soldier-founder of the great Alagoas military family almost ended soon after he had placed himself at the head of a revolution caused by opposition to the transfer of the provincial capital from the ancient city of Alagoas to Maceió. Lieutenant Colonel Fonseca, in conjunction with many citizens of Alagoas, sought

1. Gustavo Barroso, *História secreta do Brasil* (Rio de Janeiro, 1938), III, 320.

2. ''Manoel Mendes da Fonseca,'' *Encyclopedia e Dicionário Internacional*, VI (Rio de Janeiro, 1936).

3. *Ibid.*

to use political influence to prevent the government from moving the capital. The protest resulted in Fonseca's being replaced by Agostinho da Silva Neves, who was sent to Alagoas in 1839 as president of the province. On November 13, 1839, Fonseca and his troops were defeated by government forces from Bahia, Pernambuco, and the town of Maceió. Fonseca retired to Sergipe, where on December 3 he surrendered himself and was taken to Rio de Janeiro for trial. After having been imprisoned on the Ilha de Villegaignon for a few months, he was freed on May 26, 1840. The people of Alagoas demonstrated their appreciation for his effort to prevent the capital from being moved away by electing him to a public office. Six years later he was restored to his place in the army, and soon after regaining his military rank Fonseca retired to private life. He died on August 24, 1859. His wife, who was seventeen years younger than her husband, lived until 1873.[4]

Manoel Mendes and Rosa Maria Paulina da Fonseca were the parents of eight boys and two girls. Deodoro was the third child born to the couple, his older brothers Hermes Ernesto and Severiano Martins having been born in 1824 and 1825, respectively. The other children of the family were Pedro Paulino, Hippolito Mendes, Eduardo Emiliano, João Serveriano, Emilia Rosa, Amelia Rosa, and Affonso Aurelio. Seven of the boys of the family distinguished themselves in military life, and the family has been referred to by Brazilian historians as the "Seven Swords of Alagoas."[5]

Manoel Deodoro da Fonseca, the third son, at an early age indicated a desire to follow in the footsteps of his father and of his older brothers, all of whom had selected military careers. When he was sixteen he entered the Military School in Rio de Janeiro. After two years of study he was made a cadet first class on April 18, 1845. Two years later he completed the artillery course of study. In the years following his completion of the course of the Military School, Deodoro was sent to Pernambuco, where the Praieira revolution was taking place. He participated in the action of February 2, 1849, in which Nunes Machado, well-known Pernambucan liberal who was fighting with the forces that opposed the government, was killed. In this action Deodoro conducted himself courageously and thereby won the praise of his superior officers.[6] During the same year Deodoro

4. Ernesto Senna, *Deodoro, subsídios para a história* (Rio de Janeiro, 1913), p. 169.
5. "Manoel Mendes da Fonseca."
6. Augusto Tavares de Lyra, "Manoel Deodoro da Fonseca," *RIHGB*, CLV, 276.

again distinguished himself when he commanded the troops which opposed the rebels in the city of Rio Formoso. As a reward for his conduct during the conflicts in the northern provinces, he was promoted to first lieutenant of artillery on April 30, 1852.[7]

Deodoro returned to Rio de Janeiro in 1854, where, after serving several months in the fortress of Santa Cruz, he was appointed adjutant and secretary of the Battalion of Engineers, which had recently been organized.[8] He was promoted to captain in 1856 and sent to São Paulo where he served under the orders of the minister of war. Having returned to Rio de Janeiro in 1858, he was given command of the first company of students of the Military School in the Battalion of Engineers. During the same year, on April 16, 1859, he informed the Ministry of War of his marriage to Dona Mariana Cecilia de Souza Meirelles, who took as her married name Mariana Cecilia Meirelles da Fonseca. Soon after his marriage to Dona Mariana, Deodoro was sent to the province of Mato Grosso where he served under the president of the province. During this tour of duty Deodoro was praised by his commanding officer for his zeal, intelligence, and devotion to duty.[9]

Three years later Deodoro was ordered to return to Rio de Janeiro. In the fall of 1864, he embarked for the southern frontier with the First Foot Artillery Battalion, which was destined to take part in the campaign in Uruguay. After the surrender of the Uruguayan capital, Montevideo, and the signing of the Treaty of the Triple Alliance, he and his battalion were transferred to the Argentine province of Entre Rios, where they became a part of the nucleus of the allied armies which fought against the Paraguayan dictator, López. While in Entre Rios, Deodoro was promoted to major and made commander of the Second Battalion of *Voluntários da pátria*. This battalion formed the vanguard of the corps which penetrated the enemy's territory on April 16, 1866. On the day of the entry into enemy territory, the commander of the Brazilian troops, General Osorio, accompanied by a small force, advanced to the front to make a reconnaissance. He and his troops were almost immediately surrounded by the enemy and were saved by Deodoro and the Second Battalion of Volunteers. General Osorio mentioned this action in his order of the day, saying that Deodoro

7. Senna, p. 171.
8. *Ibid.*, p. 174.
9. *Ibid.*, p. 291.

was especially congratulated for calmness, courage and initiative, in directing the vangard which was composed of troops of different corps, who had already disembarked, in an intrepid advance in support of the guards of the commanding general who found themselves almost surrounded by the enemy. The enemy was forced to withdraw.[10]

Deodoro continued to demonstrate his skill and courage as a soldier during the five years of conflict which followed. He built up a legend of military valor at Itapiru, Estero Ballaco, Tuyuti, Boqueirão do Source, Potrero Obella, Taji, Establecimiento, Angustura, Itororo, Pirebebui, and Campo Grande. He advanced to the rank of lieutenant colonel on January 18, 1869, and to colonel on February 20, 1869. Deodoro's valor and military skill repeatedly won praise from his superior officers. At Estero Bellaco on May 2, 1866, and at Tuyuti on May 24, 1866, his conduct caused the commanding officer to report that "Major Manoel Deodoro da Fonseca is already so well known that it is sufficient to say of him and his corps . . . that they have been brilliant, distinguished, and noble in the performance of their duty."[11] Caxias mentioned him on October 14, 1868, in his report to the Emperor: "Lieutenant Colonel Manoel Deodoro da Fonseca is commended for his valor."[12] Deodoro was awarded the medal of the Knights of the Imperial Order of the Cross and the decoration of the Imperial Order of the Rose for his heroic conduct during these battles. When promoted to colonel on February 20, 1869, he was awarded the Medal of Military Merit on the same day that he received the promotion. By a decree of September 6, 1869, he was named a Dignitary of the Imperial Order of the Cross for his services in the actions of December, 1868, and while in the Cordilheira campaign.[13]

While Deodoro was distinguishing himself on the field of battle, six of his seven brothers were also fighting for their country. After the retirement of her husband from public life, Dona Rosa Maria Paulina da Fonseca had moved the family residence from Maceió in Alagoas to Rio de Janeiro. In Rio her home became a gathering place for those who came to the capital from Alagoas.[14] After the war with Paraguay began she saw all but one of her sons march away to the battle areas. At the suggestion of the Emperor, one of the

10. "Marechal Manoel Deodoro da Fonseca," *RIHGB*, LV, Pt. 2, 533.
11. Hermes da Fonseca Filho, *Dois grandes vultos da república* (Porto Alegre, 1935), p. 75.
12. Senna, p. 174; Fonseca Filho, p. 76.
13. "Marechal Manoel Deodoro da Fonseca," *RIHGB*, LV, Pt. 2, 535; Senna, p. 172.
14. Senna, p. 170.

younger sons, Pedro Paulino da Fonseca, was permitted to remain in Rio de Janeiro to care for the mother and for the wives of the older brothers. Pedro Paulino, with the support of his mother, soon sought active military service, but Deodoro, after a conference with some of the older brothers, opposed the entrance of the eight brothers into the army. He wrote to Pedro Paulino and informed him that should he persist in his attempt to enter the army, the other brothers would request that an officer be detached from the army to stay with the women. "It would be a fine thing," wrote Deodoro sarcastically, "for an officer of the line to leave the army in time of war to be replaced by a reserve officer!"[15]

Dona Rosa Maria was a woman of character and great courage. When she learned that negotiations were under way for peace with López, she told her friends: "I would prefer never to see my sons again, to have all of them buried in Paraguay in glorious death on the field of battle, than that our country be saved by a shameful peace."[16] During September, 1866, she received news of the death of her sons Hippolito and Affonso, who were killed in the battle at Curupaity on September 22, 1866.[17] Two years later she received news that her son Eduardo, commander of the Twenty-fourth Infantry Battalion of Volunteers, had been killed in battle at the Bridge of Itororo, December 6, 1868. Deodoro and Hermes were wounded during the same engagement.[18]

Dom Pedro, on reception of this mournful news, had sought to soften the blow to the mother. He had sent one of his courtiers with instructions to break the news as gently as possible. The courtier was unable to complete his report to the mother before she, suspecting his mission, asked: "Have I sons dead or wounded?" When he replied in the affirmative, the mother said "Well done."[19] Although she mourned the death of one son and the suffering of two others, in accordance with the customs of the Brazilians, Dona Rosa Maria decorated her home with flags, flowers, and lights, and joined in the celebration of the Battle of Curuguaity.[20]

Deodoro had been wounded by a rifle ball in the lower left side, but it was only a flesh wound, and he remained in Paraguay until the campaign was ended. The Count d'Eu, who commanded the allied

15. Fialho, p. 56.
16. Senna, p. 170.
17. Fialho, p. 57.
18. Rocha Pombo, X, 267; Senna, p. 171.
19. Lyra, p. 283.
20. Fialho, p. 57.

forces during the last phase of the campaign, commended Deodoro and recommended him highly to the Emperor for his courage and bravery on the field of battle.[21] In February, 1870, Deodoro was made commander of the district of Curuguaity by the Count d'Eu. On March 1 of that year the brigade under his command, the Eighth Infantry Brigade, was deactivated, and Deodoro was appointed commander of the First Battalion of Foot Artillery. This unit embarked at Rosario on April 29, 1870, and landed at Humayta on April 30. Soon after his arrival at Humayta Deodoro was given command of the Fourth Infantry Brigade. Later he was transferred to another unit with which he remained only a short time before being granted permission to return to Rio de Janeiro.

By a decree of October 14, 1874, Deodoro was promoted to brigadier general.[22] During December of the same year, he was appointed commander of the frontiers of Quarahim and Livramento in Rio Grande do Sul. On November 22, 1875, he was named inspector of the cavalry companies of the provinces of Bahia and Pernambuco, and of the Second, Seventh, Ninth, and Sixteenth Battalions of Infantry and of the Depot of Instruction of Light Infantry and Cavalry. He returned to Rio de Janeiro from Rio Grande do Sul on March 23, 1876, to begin his new tour of duty.[23] Four years later Deodoro was named commandant of the military forces of the province of Bahia. On June 30, 1880, he was relieved of this command and returned to his former post of inspector of arms. In 1883 he was named commandant of arms of the province of Rio Grande do Sul, and later in the year he was relieved of this post and made inspector of arms in the provinces of Santa Catharina, São Paulo, and Parana.

During the war years, while Manoel Deodoro da Fonseca and thousands of Brazilian officers and soldiers fought nobly for their country, and during the postwar years while the army was being neglected, the struggle was intensified between the politicians, who controlled the government, and the military, who held the power. The fall of the Zacarias cabinet because of its failure to co-operate with the Duke of Caxias, who commanded the army, alarmed the politicians, and at the same time it demonstrated to the military the effective influence they could bring to bear upon the government.

The position of the military as a deciding factor in the formation of the country's policies had its foundations in the past. The army

21. Lyra, p. 294.
22. Rocha Pombo, IX, 295.
23. "Manoel Mendes da Fonseca."

had been the deciding factor when independence was won, when Dom Pedro I was forced to abdicate, and when the majority of Dom Pedro II was proclaimed. After 1848, when internal order was restored, the army had lost much of its influence. The war against Rosas, the "Christie Question," and the threatening attitude of López during the years preceding the Paraguayan War had caused a revival of interest in the army and navy. After the war, the army, having flexed its muscles in Paraguay, observed the power of the military of the Rio de la Plata republics;[24] and guided by the new political theories learned from the professors in the military schools, it sought to make a place for itself in the political life of Brazil.

It was not difficult for an officer of the Brazilian army to enter politics. He was legally eligible to occupy a political office while on active duty with the army. The Caxias-Zacarias conflict had been the result of political alliances and entanglements. Caxias, the Conservative general, led the army, and Zacarias, the Liberal leader of the government, could not refrain from seeking to annoy and humiliate his political enemy. The imperial solution of the conflict changed it to the extent that from 1868, the year of the fall of the Zacarias cabinet, to 1889, the year of the fall of the empire, the conflict was no longer one between Liberal and Conservative parties, but one between the military and its civilian foes.

Upon the return of the soldiers from the war, each of the parties had sought to draw the generals of most prestige into its group. The Republican party, which had been organized on December 3, 1870, was young and weak. It was unable to attract any of the glittering swords of the victorious generals, but its theories were acceptable to many of the younger officers. The Liberal party had selected General Osorio, and the Conservatives basked in the reflected prestige of Caxias, the great general of their party. By 1880, both these famous commanders had died and the two major parties had made new selections. Correa da Camara, Viscount of Pelotas, who had been a leader of the cavalry during the war, replaced Osorio for the Liberals, and the Conservatives turned to General Deodoro.[25]

This gravitation of the political parties to the army leaders was not caused by love or admiration for the military. When the *politico* entered the barracks "and waved the red flag of military rights before the armed class, he did not do this with the intent to better the condition of that class."[26] He went there to secure alliances which he

24. Nabuco, *Um estadista do império*, II, 189.
25. Monteiro, *Pesquisas e depoimentos* . . . , p. 117.
26. *Contribuições*, p. 856.

could use as a tool to combat his political opponents. The officer of the army, encouraged by his civilian allies, entered politics with one particular liability. His attempt to acquire the character of the *político* and to retain that of an army officer was completely incompatible with the mores of the Brazilian political scene. The soldier, who must always uphold his reputation for courage and honor, was not suited for the civilian political struggles wherein "There is only one dominant sentiment: hatred of the opponent. In this code of morals, there is only one supreme duty: the obligation to injure and defame." There was no code of ethics in dealing with the political opponent. What was important was to deny all, even the elements of life, to the opponent. The adversary was a kind of outlaw who must be liquidated, whether in honor or in body.[27] Nabuco compared the struggle between the parties of the empire to similar conflict in the United States during the same period. He wrote that "The politician is delivered without pity to the reporters. . . . The contest is not carried out on the basis of ideas but on that of personal reputation."[28]

The insults which were addressed to members of the opposing parties applied to civilian and military opponents alike. Hence, the entrance into politics of the soldier, with his sense of honor which would not permit him to accept insult, brought a new and dangerous element into political affairs. By 1883 the abolitionist and Republican movements and the diffusion of the Positivist doctrine had produced compromising attitudes among many of the younger officers. Membership in political parties frequently caused these officers to engage in heated debate with representatives of the opposing parties, deputies, senators, and ministers. In these conflicts the spirit of the military class soon revealed itself and the personal nature of the contest took on the delicate character of a class question. That is, an army officer who engaged in a political conflict with a civilian could, in most instances, be assured of the support of the other members of his class.

The first incident demonstrating the friction between the military and the politicians occurred in January, 1883. Dr. Carlos Affonso de Assis Figueredo, civilian minister of war, had Colonel Frias Villars imprisoned as punishment for a breach of discipline.[29] This incident received little attention from the press and served only

27. *Ibid.*, p. 849.
28. Joaquim Nabuco, *Minha formação* (Rio de Janeiro, 1934), p. 137.
29. *Jornal do Comércio* (Sept. 7, 1922), p. 400.

as an irritating factor to the military who gave scant indication of their resentment. Early in the decade 1880-1890, the Conservative ministries, which were opposed to any change in the Rio Branco Law for the slow abolition of slavery, found occasion to censure and even to punish officers and cadets in the military schools who were frequently outspoken in their opposition to slavery.[30]

During 1883 Senator Marquis de Paranaguá, a Conservative and a personal friend of the Emperor, proposed a law which would establish a fund for the payment of subsistence to retired soldiers or to their widows. The fund would be maintained by obligatory payments from the soldiers while they were in active service. At first glance the proposal seemed a very worthy one, but an examination of the proposed plan revealed that it contained certain highly disturbing provisions. Under certain conditions the payments could be withheld from the soldier or from his widow. In addition to the possible loss of benefits, another provision of the plan was that ''The government will no longer be permitted to make awards of pecuniary value to its employees: and, when the good of the public service demands it, they will be retired or dismissed.''[31] This last provision of the plan would have served as a constant threat to the army officers, who, had the plan become law, would have had to obey the politicians or be discharged from the service. The proposed law was also unconstitutional in that it violated Article 149 of the Brazilian Constitution, which stated that ''Officers of the army and navy can not be deprived of their ranks except by a sentence of a competent court.''[32]

When the students of the Military School of Rio de Janeiro learned of the proposed law, they formed a directory to discuss the question in the newspapers. Lieutenant Colonel Senna Madureira, a former Brazilian military attaché in Berlin and a veteran of the Paraguayan War, was elected president of the directory. Madureira published a series of articles in the *Jornal do Comércio* in which he pointed out and analyzed the objective of the Marquis of Paranagua's proposal. He said that the project was a strong attack against the military, who, through it, would be presented with a Trojan horse (*presente de grego*).[33] The attack launched against the proposed law was successful. The directory received the support of other military schools, of army officers, and of some of the generals. The measure was suppressed at the next meeting of the Parliament and was not

30. Calogeras, p. 263.
31. Fialho, p. 48.
32. *Ibid.*, p. 49.
33. *Ibid.*

even discussed by the senators. Soon after the Senate refused further discussion of Paranagua's proposal, and perhaps because of this refusal, the government renewed the ministerial prohibition of discussion of political or military affairs in the newspapers by officers of the army or of the navy.[34]

In April, 1884, Lieutenant Colonel Madureira once more aroused the anger of his superior officers. Madureira at that time was the commandant of the Artillery School of Compo Grande, which, like many of the other military schools in Brazil, was a focal point of abolitionist propaganda. The arrival of an abolitionist *jangada*,[35] the *Francisco do Nascimento*, from Ceará, an imperial province which had freed most of its slaves, had been the occasion for a great demonstration on the part of the personnel of that school.[36] The minister of war, upon reading in the *Gazeta da Tarde* that the arrival of the craft had been celebrated by the personnel of the school, had the adjutant general order Madureira to report immediately on the correctness of the information in the newspaper. Madureira, in a letter to the adjutant general, stated that he was unable to recognize the competency of the adjutant general to inquire about the events which occurred within the school. He then informed the adjutant general that because he was "subordinate to the Count d'Eu, Commanding General of Artillery, I have no intention of responding to your letter."[37] Madureira was dismissed from the command of the Artillery School and reprimanded in an order of the day by the minister of war. The adjutant general had asked that he be punished "for the good of the discipline of the army."[38]

In 1885 the rise of the reactionary Conservative Cotegipe to the presidency of the cabinet aroused the abolitionists, who now found themselves increasingly supported by the military. Among the edu-

34. Galanti, V, 97.
35. ''The Jangada resembles nothing I have ever seen before: six or eight logs are made fast together by two traverse beams; at one end there is a raised seat, on which a man (*the Jangadeiro*) placed himself to steer, for they are furnished with a sort of rudder; sometimes the seat is large enough to admit two sitters, another bench at the foot of a mast, immense for the size of a raft, holds clothes and provisions, or an upright pole is fixed in one of the logs, to which these things are suspended, and a large triangular sail of cotton cloth completes the *jangada*, in which the hardy Brazilian sailor ventures to sea, the waves constantly washing over it, and carries cargoes of cotton, or other goods, or, in case of necessity, letters and despatches, hundreds of miles in safety.'' Maria Dundas Graham Callcott, *Journal of a Voyage to Brazil* (London, 1824), p. 99.
36. Monteiro, *Pesquisas e depoimentos* . . . , p. 124; Fialho, p. 50; *Jornal do Comércio* (Sept. 7, 1922), p. 400.
37. Rocha Pombo, X, 54; Fleiuss, *História Administrativa*, p. 412.
38. Rocha Pombo, X, 54; Monteiro, *Pesquisas e depoimentos* . . . , p. 124.

cated officers there seemed to be a definite antipathy toward the government.[39] Any pretext could unite the spirits of these opponents of the monarchy and lead them to make serious trouble for the government. The pretext was furnished through the criticism made of the inspection of an isolated infantry company by Colonel Cunha Mattos.

Colonel Cunha Mattos, in his report of the inspection of the company, told of important irregularities in the uniforms of the soldiers. He recommended that a council be named to investigate and determine the responsibility for these irregularities and that Captain Pedro José de Lima, commander of the company, who seemed to be responsible, be relieved of his command. He also recommended that the council be composed of men who were not residents of the district so that politics would not be permitted to influence the findings of the council.

Four months after the inspection had been made, Captain Lima, who commanded the company which had been found delinquent, sent a complaint to Minister of War Alfredo Chaves, charging that Colonel Cunha Mattos had made a hasty inspection, and that he had failed to denounce his friends who were responsible for the condition of the troops. The minister of war, on receipt of the charges made by the captain against Colonel Cunha Mattos, ordered that the captain appear before a Council of War. A few days later a member of the House of Deputies, Simplicio Coelho de Rezende, a personal friend of Captain Lima, spoke before the members of the House of Deputies and publicly advised the minister to proceed carefully. He pointed out that Chaves was not familiar with the duties of his office and that it was necessary to warn him so that he might avoid being placed in a compromising position. He added that "the military who concern themselves with politics, not only know the rules of strategy, but also have the craftiness of a vixen."[40]

The deputy's comments were printed in the newspapers, and Colonel Cunha Mattos, reading the statement, became offended. He remarked that he was not inclined to bear the insults which the irresponsible deputy was directing at him and he made an allusion to the friendship which existed between Coelho de Rezende and the accused captain. Simplicio, after reading the remarks of Cunha Mattos in the press, heaped further insults upon the colonel, saying that he had been captured in Paraguay, and that while "a prisoner of López he had directed enemy artillery fire against Brazilian troops."[41]

39. Rocha Pombo, X, 55; Barroso, *História secreta* . . . , III, 314.
40. Rocha Pombo, X, 54; *Contribuições*, p. 851.
41. Rocha Pombo, X, 55.

Colonel Cunha Mattos asked that Simplicio give him an opportunity to prove that he was no coward, and he wrote several articles in which he defended himself. In one of them he asserted that the charge by Coelho de Rezende was the result of an error made by the minister of war in the interpretation of the information in his report.[42] Chaves, considering this statement a breach of discipline, ordered that the colonel be detained forty-eight hours in the waiting room of his regimental headquarters. This occurred near the end of July, 1886. The action of the minister of war in this case was not unusual. It was designed to maintain the prestige of his office. The minister justified his action on the basis of the colonel's report. In addition to this he reminded his critics that on December 26, 1884, an *aviso* (military administrative regulation) had been issued by Candido de Oliveira, a Liberal minister of war and a member of the Dantas cabinet, approving an order of the day of the adjutant general which prohibited officers from discussing political or military affairs in the press without the approval of the minister of war. Precedence in the matter was in favor of the minister's action; an *aviso* of October 4, 1859, signed by Sebastião do Rego Barros, himself a member of the military class and at that time minister of war, had stated that "All officers who go to the newspapers in order to provoke conflicts and disrespect of their superiors deserve the most severe censure."[43] By an *aviso* of October 9, 1882, Carlos Affonso had reminded Colonel Mattos himself that he should observe the *aviso* of 1859. In 1855, the minister of war, another Liberal, had directed the attention of the military to the previous *avisos* concerning public discussion of military and political problems without consent of the minister of war.

These factors, which seemed to bolster the minister's action, made little impact upon the military. Alfredo Chaves was a civilian, and the military saw in the punishment of Cunha Mattos an indorsement of the charges made by Coelho de Rezende in the House of Deputies. The personal conflict between the officer and the two politicians developed into a conflict between the military class and the bureaucrats of the government.

Viscount Pelotas, senator from Rio Grande do Sul and a leader of cavalry in the Paraguayan War, rose in the Senate to defend his friend Colonel Cunha Mattos. Pelotas, expressing surprise at the punishment to which the colonel had been subjected, declared that

42. Fialho, p. 46; *Jornal do Comércio* (Sept. 7, 1922), p. 400.
43. Rocha Pombo, X, 56.

"the officers of the army should see in that which their comrade has suffered an insult to all of them."[44] Continuing his speech, Pelotas added: "An officer who is wounded in his honor has the undeniable right to avenge himself."[45] Senator Barros Barreto, of Pernambuco, referring to the *avisos* which limited military use of the newspapers without permission in such circumstances, interposed, "Yes, if the laws permit this."[46] Pelotas, in a manner which indicated "the contempt which the military felt for the civilian politician,"[47] answered:

I do not say that our laws permit it; I am telling the noble Minister of War what I understand an officer should do when he is insulted, and, be it known to the noble Senator from Pernambuco, that he, who is speaking, would proceed in such a manner, without considering what the law forbids. I place my honor above everything.[48]

One can imagine the effect of the words of the old and respected general on the officers of the army. During the following years when the military question entered its most acute stage, Baron Cotegipe, president of the cabinet, attributed to Pelotas the major responsibility for the conflict. "A seed produced a great tree and the words of Pelotas have been the seed of the question."[49] The man in whose defense Pelotas had spoken accepted his punishment without complaint.

The conflict between Cunha Mattos and the two civilians precipitated many heated speeches in the Senate. Senator Franco de Sá, who had been minister of war at the time of the visit of the abolitionist *jangada* to the Campo Grande Artillery School, made allusions to that incident in a discourse to the Senate. He said that the dismissal of the school's commandant, Lieutenant Colonel Madureira, had been a punishment for that officer's failure to show proper respect to the adjutant general.[50] The incident to which the senator referred, unlike the case of Cunha Mattos, was of political origin. Madureira, commandant of the school, an abolitionist and a Republican, upon the arrival of the *jangada* had permitted a demonstration to be made which benefitted the followers of his political party. The minister of war, Franco de Sá, was an opponent of both abolition and Republicanism; consequently, he had used the means at his disposal to attack Madureira, his political opponent. In the opinion of the

44. *Ibid.; Contribuições*, p. 851.
45. *Contribuições*, p. 851.
46. *Ibid.*
47. *Ibid.*
48. *Ibid.*
49. Rocha Pombo, X, 56.
50. Fialho, p. 50.

minister, Madureira ought to be subject to the attacks of his political opponents, despite his rank. Madureira and his Republican, military, and abolitionist comrades disagreed; in their opinion the honor of the uniform had been sullied. "They did not see in these natural occurances the penalties to which those who place their nose in politics are subjected; they see an offense to the honor of the uniform."[51]

At the time of the Cunha Mattos incident, Madureira was commandant of the Artillery School of Rio Pardo in Rio Grande do Sul. The statements of Franco de Sá concerning the *jangada* incident of 1884 were published in the newspapers of Rio Grande do Sul, and the volatile officer, reading them, became angered and sought to defend himself. If the former minister of war sought to provoke a new incident, his selection of Madureira as an opponent was an excellent one. During the Paraguayan War, the Duke of Caxias had referred to this officer as an intelligent soldier who had shown valor, but the great general had added that Madureira was very insubordinate.[52] During 1878, while returning from duty as military attaché in Berlin, Madureira had provoked an incident with a French official on board a French packet, causing the intervention of the commander of the ship. The government of Brazil later regarded the conduct of the ship's commander as justifiable. Nevertheless, Madureira was regarded as a brilliant military man. A supporter of Republican and abolitionist ideas, he was highly regarded by his fellow officers, particularly by the younger officers and those who were graduates of the military schools.

Madureira defended himself against the charges of Franco de Sá by publishing justifications for his action in the press. His statement first appeared in the *Federação* of Rio Grande do Sul. Later it was reprinted in the *Jornal do Comércio* of Rio de Janeiro. Madureira denied having offended the adjutant general and charged that his dismissal had been the result of political opposition and personal jealousy by the former minister of war.

Alfredo Chaves, minister of war in the Cotegipe cabinet, censured Madureira on September 4, 1886, for having disobeyed the *aviso* which prohibited officers from discussing publicly the affairs of the administration without the previous permission of the minister of war.[53] Discussing this censure with a friend, Madureira said, "On reading it in the newspaper I was filled with indignation at that

51. *Contribuições*, p. 852.
52. *Ibid.*, p. 853; Rocha Pombo, X, 58; Monteiro, *Pesquisas e depoimentos* . . . , p. 132.
53. Monteiro, *Pesquisas e depoimentos* . . . , p. 130.

humiliation which the minister had inflicted upon me.''[54] Madureira wrote a protest, dated September 23, 1886, which was published in the newspapers of the cities of the empire. In the statement released to the press, Madureira asked that he be relieved of his duties at the Artillery School and stated that he protested in the name of the pride, honor, and dignity of the military class against the ideas of the minister of war and the unusual theories which he sought to bring to bear upon the army.

In which law, in which disciplinary regulation [asked Madureira] does the Conselheiro Alfredo Chaves find authority to reprimand in a most severe manner, an officer who has been attacked in that which he holds most precious, his reputation as an officer, for having defended himself against the false charges of a senator of the empire?[55]

Madureira then charged that the minister of war could not cite any legal prohibition to a military man's defending himself when his honor was questioned. He stated that the minister could reprimand him as many times as he wished, but added ''that for such an honorable motive I shall always be prepared to justify myself before a Council of War as to the legality of my procedure.''[56] The protest concluded with the harsh words that ''when a competent authority passes a law forbidding the military to defend themselves against a member of parliament, who seemingly has the exclusive privilege of inflicting insults, on that day, I shall leave the ranks of the army.''[57]

The protest was quickly transferred to many parts of the empire and aroused the emotions of the military class. It was particularly effective in the province in which Madureira was stationed at the time. Rio Grande do Sul had been a center of revolutionary disturbances for almost a century. Because of its proximity to the Rio de la Plata republics which frequently underwent periods of disorder, a large military force was maintained there. This proximity also permitted the easy infiltration of *caudillo* ideas, and the peoples of the province shared the republican sentiments of their neighbors across the border.[58] Consequently, it was not surprising that Madureira received overwhelming support from the officers stationed in Rio Grande do Sul. Moreover, telegraph messages of congratulation were sent to him by officers from all the garrisons of Brazil.

The Viscount of Pelotas, who had been a lieutenant general in

54. Fialho, p. 51.
55. *Ibid.*, p. 52.
56. *Ibid.*, p. 53.
57. *Ibid.*
58. *Ibid.*, p. 62.

the Paraguayan War, in a letter to a Republican newspaper of his native province, Rio Grande do Sul, thanked the editor for his sympathy and words of appreciation in the Madureira case. In this letter Pelotas said that the government seemed determined to destroy what the army guarded with the greatest zeal—its honor.

Yesterday, it was Colonel Cunha Mattos who was confined to the headquarters of his regiment for having repelled an offense to his honor. . . . Today, it is Lieutenant Colonel Madureira, admired in the army for his bravery, illustrious and dedicated to the service, a man whom the government has entrusted with a commission of the highest confidence . . . who is severly reprimanded because he dares to clarify a question which could cast doubt upon his feelings of subordination and respect to an illustrious general.[59]

The viscount then asked the ominous question, "Who will it be tomorrow?" Pelotas complimented the army, not only for demonstrating its valor on the field of battle, but for showing even more valor by its acceptance with resignation of the inconsiderate action of the government. These insults were being heaped upon those "who tomorrow might have to fight heroically in the defense of their country."[60] The letter concluded with the hope that the incredible action of the government would not continue. This letter was given wide publicity and it further aroused the spirit of the military class.

Marshal Manoel Deodoro da Fonseca in 1883 had been sent to Rio Grande do Sul as commander of the military force there. At the time of the publication of the Madureira protest he was the acting president of the province as well as commander of the military force. Immediately after the publication of the Madureira protest, the adjutant general sent a telegram to Marshal Deodoro asking if he had given permission for that officer to publish his protest.[61] In response to the telegram from the adjutant general, Deodoro said that he would deal with the matter immediately.[62] Having formally heard the case, he informed the adjutant general that "Madureira was justified in defending himself against the accusations of Senator Franco de Sá."[63] Deodoro's reply indicated that although he was a member of the Conservative party, his loyalty to the military class transcended all party allegiances.

Cotegipe, president of the cabinet in 1885, had urged the Baron

59. *Ibid.*
60. *Ibid.*
61. Galanti, V, 99; Fialho, p. 59; Fleiuss, *História administrativa*, p. 413; Monteiro, *Pesquisas e depoimentos* . . . , p. 134.
62. Senna, p. 252.
63. *Ibid.*, p. 253.

of Lucena, who was departing for Rio Grande do Sul, to become acquainted with Deodoro, as the latter would become president of the province whenever the baron was absent. Cotegipe added that Deodoro was a brave man and that he was destined to take the place in the army left vacant by the death of the Duke of Caxias. Soon after the publication of Pelotas' letter, Deodoro, who had been a political opponent of this liberal general, renewed friendship with him. The two officers met in one of the churches of Porto Alegre, at the celebration of a Mass for the great Brazilian general, Osorio, under whom both had served in Paraguay. The generals embraced cordially and pledged unity in opposing civilian encroachment upon the privileges and rights of the military class.[64]

The publication of the protest of Lieutenant Colonel Madureira and the support which he obtained from his fellow officers intensified the conflict between the civilian government officials and the military. The animosities aroused by this conflict culminated in the fall of the monarchy and the establishment of the republic. However, as the following chapter will indicate, the events leading to the fall of the monarchy were influenced by factors other than the conflict between the military class and the civilians.

64. Fialho, p. 63; Galanti, V, 99; Monteiro, *Pesquisas e depoímentos* . . . , p. 144.

Chapter Four

Other Factors of Imperial Disintegration: Abolition, the Conflict with the Church, and Republicanism

Of the other factors contributing to imperial disintegration, abolition has been the one most frequently cited by historians of this era. The abolitionist movement, which became fused with the Republican movement, provided the altruistic motive for the establishment of a new regime. After the war with Paraguay the abolitionist movement was intensified.

The sponsors of the Rio Branco Law of gradual emancipation in 1871 had hoped that his measure would quiet the demands for abolition and that the *fazendeiros* would be content. Gradual emancipation would be less likely to drive them to revolt than would immediate emancipation. But the abolitionists were not content with the Rio Branco Law, and seven years after its passage new and skilful advocates of complete abolition appeared. Led by Joaquim Nabuco, son of a wealthy and aristocratic Pernambucan family and one of the most sagacious men of the last years of the empire, these reformers brushed aside the economic effect of abolition and placed the arguments against slavery on a religious, humanitarian, and philosophical plane.[1] By his persuasive speeches Nabuco began to stir the leaders of the Brazilian middle class. "He invoked principles long forgotten or ignored—the dignity of human life, the bonds of Christian brotherhood, the immortality of the souls of those unjustly condemned to a life of cruel servitude."[2]

When the Liberals returned to power in 1878, many of their ✓

1. Duque-Estrada, p. 23; Calmon, *História social do Brasil*, II, 395; Percy Alvin Martin, "Slavery and Abolition in Brazil," *Hispanic American Historical Review*, XIII, 180.
2. Calogeras, p. 253.

leaders felt much as the Conservatives did about abolition. For them it was a question which had been settled by the Rio Branco Law. Silveira Martins, a leader of the Liberal party, in replying to those who demanded changes in that law, said:

I understand that these are righteous ideas, but they are inopportune. There is nothing more justifiable than the emancipation of the slaves; however, Senhores, who would dare to decree a measure which would instantly be the death blow of labor and of industry, the mortification, the destruction and ruin of this vast Empire![3]

Abolitionists pointed out that the law which ended the slave trade in 1850, far from adversely affecting the national economy, had been beneficial to it. Production increased rapidly because the capital which had been diverted to the importation of slaves was expended, after the passage of that law, in new commercial ventures. The fears of the opponents of emancipation seemed groundless before the penetrating logic of Nabuco, who in condemnation of them said to a friend: "As long as we have slavery of both men and of the franchise we shall continue to be, as we are today, scorned by the civilized world, which cannot understand why so little is produced from a land so rich in natural resources."[4]

Demands for abolition in the House of Deputies increased during the spring of 1879, and from the galleries spectators applauded the abolitionist deputies. But in the face of the Liberal-Conservative joint opposition, the abolitionists modified their demands and assailed the unsavory aspect of the traffic in slaves between the provinces. An act which would have prohibited the transportation of slaves from one province to another for the purpose of sale was proposed in the legislature, but it was defeated. This proposal would have been a heavy blow to the forces of slavery because the development of the coffee industry in the southern provinces and the decline of the sugar and cotton industries in the north had created a surplus of slave labor in the north. Consequently, northern slaveowners had been selling their surplus slaves to the southern coffee planters. The opposition pointed out that the Rio Branco Law had settled the emancipation problem and that to attempt to emancipate the million slaves in Brazil at that time would cost millions of dollars. Such a move would be harmful to the entire economy of the country. The Conservative-Liberal leadership, in order to end the argument, agreed that no further discussion of slavery would be permitted.[5]

3. *Contribuições*, p. 665.
4. Nabuco, *Um estadista do império*, III, 143.
5. *Contribuições*, p. 666.

Discussion of emancipation could be prevented or limited in the chambers of the House of Deputies, but outside those chambers the movement against slavery was intensified.[6] The Brazilian Anti-Slavery Society was founded by Nabuco in 1880.[7] The newspapers of Bahia and those of the northern provinces refused to print announcements of the sale of slaves. And within the chambers of the House of Deputies it became almost impossible to silence the proponents of abolition. Nabuco considered that the position of his party was unworthy of a party of initiative and progress. He led the opposition against the gag rule on discussion of abolition in the House of Deputies.

After Saraiva replaced Sinimbu as president of the cabinet, the chief interest of the new cabinet was the reform of the procedure for election of deputies. This interest was temporarily put aside when Nabuco confronted the new ministry with the demand for complete abolition at the end of the ten-year period 1880-1890. The response from the leader of the new government was: "The present ministry does not recognize this question of slavery."[8] Many of the Liberals in the House of Deputies supported the views of Nabuco but took no action in favor of them because they regarded the question of direct election as of more importance. Dom Pedro II also gave precedence to the direct election project. In the contest over which question should receive precedence, Nabuco obtained the support of eighteen deputies, but the opposition received eighty votes. Despite evident popular support outside the halls of the legislature and the support of such prominent newspapers as the *Jornal do Comércio* and the *Gazeta de Noticias*, Nabuco's proposal received little consideration from the representatives of the Brazilian people.

Saraiva, commenting on Nabuco's proposal, said that he understood the need for complete abolition at an early date, but he considered that direct election and abolition could not be considered at one time. In postponing the question in this manner he did not forget the lot of the freed slave in Brazil. The reform gave the franchise to all eligible Brazilians without distinction of color. He also indicated his attitude concerning abolition when, discussing emancipation with a friend, Marcolino Moura, he said, "Should I be minister again, it can be."[9]

6. Evaristo de Moraes, "Pedro II e o movimento abolicionista," *RIHGB*, CLII, 335.
7. Duque-Estrada, p. 88; Martin, "Slavery and Abolition . . . ," p. 182.
8. *Contribuições*, p. 668; Pereira da Silva, *Memórias do meu tempo*, II, 215.
9. *Contribuições*, p. 671.

Saraiva was a man of action but he preferred to act when the time was opportune. The question of emancipation in 1880 was a source of bitter feelings. The provinces of the north were selling their slaves to the southern provinces and at the same time were becoming strongly abolitionist. And in the northern parts of Brazil the people were beginning to refer to the southern provinces as slavocracies. Such a situation created ill-will and could have been dangerous.[10]

The abolitionists next proposed that slaves less than forty-nine years old born in Angola, Loanda, and Mozambique be emancipated. If they had not been born in Brazil and if they were less than forty-nine years of age, they had been imported in violation of the law of 1831, which forbade further importation of slaves into Brazil.

Frequent abolition conferences in Rio de Janeiro were attended by many members of the upper classes. Felicio dos Santos observed that abolition had become a social movement. Belfort Duarte, opponent of abolition, asked the government if it approved the propaganda for abolition, the public meetings, the political banquets, and even the remarks made by the American minister when he attended one of the banquets.

After the passage of the election reform on January 9, 1881, the election which followed was one of the most democratic in the history of the empire. Youthful, idealistic, and patriotic men, filled with ideas of progress, appeared in the House of Deputies. Joaquim Nabuco, the tireless proponent of emancipation, was defeated, but leadership in the House of Deputies was placed in the able hands of one of the newly elected deputies, Affonso Celso, Jr.

Martinho Campos, leader of the new ministry, was an opponent of emancipation, and his statement regarding the proponents of abolition was one of the most hostile of the period:

Among those who show interest in this question there are two types of zeal. There is that of the philosophical men, sincere and true, who are moved only by feelings of kindness. None of them is able to do more than what has been done for the slaves. There is, also, a group, who, finding no other political means to disturb the government, use the question as a means of opposition. To the first group we extend sympathy; all the respect and aid of the government. The second group merits the aid, protection and support accorded vandals, enemies of the society.[11]

10. *Ibid.*
11. *Ibid.*, p. 673.

Replying to an assertion that the nation demanded abolition, Martinho Campos asked, "How does one know the opinion of the Nation? Is it by what a half dozen youths or old maniacs write in the newspapers?"[12]

It was obvious that nothing could be expected of the new ministry, and the abolitionists intensified their efforts in other directions. As a result of their influence many provinces passed laws prohibiting inter-provincial traffic in slaves. In Ceará, boatmen (*jangadeiros*) aroused by abolitionist sentiments refused to use their crafts for inter-provincial transportation of slaves.[13] Since their boats were the only vessels capable of passing the heavy breakers outside northern harbors, their refusal to transport slaves for purposes of sale practically ended the slave trade in coastal regions. The Liberator Society of Fortaleza, composed of the shopkeepers of that city, supported the boatmen, and their joint declaration, "No slaves embark from this port!" was enforced.[14]

On May 24, 1883, Paranaguá was replaced by Lafayette as president of the cabinet, but the Speech from the Throne, to the chagrin of the abolitionists, continued as in preceding years to emphasize the gradual extinction of the servile element in accordance with the provisions of the Rio Branco Law. The abolitionists now felt a need for action. During the previous ministry it had been necessary to transfer the Fifteenth Infantry Battalion from Ceará to Pará to prevent disorder within the battalion because of abolitionist propaganda. Now the *Liberator*, a newspaper of Fortaleza, was violently outspoken in its demands for abolition. The officers of the transferred battalion had organized a Military Abolitionist Club, which elected as its president an army surgeon.[15] The club had encouraged the flight of slaves from their owners' plantations, and it had even given them protection after their flight. The public law enforcement agencies of the province could not be counted upon to protect the property of the slaveowners. This was the situation which confronted the Lafayette cabinet.[16]

Abolition orators pointed out that 30,940 slaves had been liberated by their owners. In their opinion this indicated that the government's action in liberating the slaves was much too slow. To those who opposed emancipation because of fear of the effect upon the economy

12. *Ibid.*
13. Duque-Estrada, p. 112.
14. Calogeras, p. 255.
15. Duque-Estrada, p. 113.
16. Martin, "Slavery and Abolition . . . ," p. 185.

of the country, they pointed to the progress of Ceará. That province, having sold or liberated most of its slaves, found that with the use of free labor its exports had quadrupled.[17] Sentiment for complete abolition advanced enthusiastically in the newspapers, in clubs, in the army, and in the courts, but the legislative houses and the government failed to heed the demands of the people. This increased agitation provoked a reaction from the slaveowners. In Pernambuco and in other provinces they formed clubs and agrarian leagues for defense against abolitionist propaganda. Party lines were ignored in the membership of these organizations, for even as members of both great political parties were found among the abolitionists, so also did they mix freely in the anti-abolition clubs.[18]

The year 1883 passed without any change having been made in the Rio Branco Law, but the agitation against slavery continued to increase. The Speech from the Throne of 1884 was a replica of those of other years: the problem was to be solved by development of the law of 1871.[19] But the movement against slavery had reached such proportions that the *Jornal do Comércio* commented that "We are witnessing the funeral rites of slavery."[20] Dom Pedro II was keenly aware of the growing demand for abolition and he was only awaiting an opportune moment to intervene in favor of it. In 1888, Hector Varella, a journalist from Buenos Aires who had visited Rio de Janeiro during 1883, wrote that Dom Pedro had informed him that "None of my fellow citizens desire abolition more ardently than I."[21]

On March 24, 1884, the *Gazeta da Tarde*, an abolitionist newspaper of Rio de Janeiro, published the following telegram: "Fortaleza, . . . We have won the first battle. Inform the emperor, whose abolitionist sentiments we respect, that despite persecution from the government, Ceará is free."[22] The telegram was signed by eight of the abolitionist leaders of that province. In Rio de Janeiro a carnival was held to celebrate the abolition of slavery in Ceará. Parades, during which the Libertadora Cearense and the *jangadeiros* were singled out for honors, were a feature of the celebration which lasted from March 25 until April 3. The event was also greeted with appropriate joy in Ceará.

17. Affonso de Carvalho, ''Abolicionismo e democracia nas Arcadas, ''*Revista do Instituto Histórico e Geográfico de São Paulo*, XXXII, 358.
18. *Contribuições*, p. 681.
19. *Ibid.*, p. 683.
20. *Ibid.*; Galanti, V, 40.
21. *Contribuições*, p. 683.
22. Duque-Estrada, p. 116.

The abolitionist movement depended for its success on the tireless efforts of deeply committed Brazilians who were able to marshal opinion both at home and abroad. Ruy Barbosa, son of a Bahian physician and himself an eloquent orator and skilled writer, devoted many years of his life in unremitting endeavor to win emancipation for the slaves. José do Patrocinio, of slave descent and a violent abolitionist, carried the struggle to the continent of Europe. After the slaves had been freed in Ceará, he gave a banquet for the journalists of Paris, seeking to give the Brazilian abolitionist cause further propaganda. He also wrote to Victor Hugo, informing him that one law had declared that no more slaves would be born in Brazil and that "Thanks to the efforts of the abolitionists, in Ceara another law will be made, —no more slaves will die in my country."[23] Propaganda in foreign countries was an important source of pressure against slavery: "That which gave such intensity to the abolitionist ideal and contributed powerfully to the climax of exaltation to which it finally attained, was the pressure of foreign example acting upon a race which is imaginative, susceptible to idealism, and richly endowed with enthusiasm."[24]

During 1883 the Confederation of Abolitionists, consisting of a union of all of the abolitionist societies of Brazil, was organized. Under the leadership of an executive committee the propaganda against slavery increased rapidly. The movement did not confine itself to propaganda but took direct action to end slavery. Slaves were kidnapped and sent by ship to Ceará, "the land of light"; arriving off the coast of that province they were landed by the *jangadeiros*.[25] False manumission papers were distributed among the slaves. A slave could easily secure his freedom on presentation of these papers to a sympathetic magistrate.

The politician who desired to maintain the status quo began to realize that consideration of the question could not safely continue to be ignored.[26] When Manoel Pinto de Souza Dantas became president of the ministry on June 6, 1884, he proposed that slaves over sixty years of age be freed without compensation to their owners, that the emancipation fund be increased, that inter-provincial slave traffic be prohibited, and that the value of slaves in different age groups be determined by a registration.[27]

23. *Ibid.*, p. 119.
24. Vianna, *Occaso do império* (São Paulo, 1925), p. 70; Martin, "Slavery and Abolition . . . ," p. 173.
25. Duque-Estrada, p. 121.
26. Galanti, V, 47.
27. Monteiro, *Pesquisas e depoimentos* . . ., p. 110; Duque-Estrada, p. 31.

The slaveowners in the legislative chambers bitterly denounced the Dantas proposal. Dom Pedro himself was attacked because he appeared to favor it.[28] The opponents of the measure secured enough support to force Dantas to resign. Saraiva was called upon to organize the new ministry, and he too fell because of the same opposition. It seemed that the Dantas proposal could obtain no support in Parliament, but that outside the legislative halls the advocates of abolition clamored for such a measure. In the face of their pressure, Baron Cotegipe's Conservative ministry secured the passage of a measure which contained most of the provisions of the Dantas project, the only difference being that slaves sixty years of age were free, but had to serve their owners an additional three years.[29]

It would seem that each effort to satisfy the abolitionists only increased their desire for extinction of slavery in Brazil. Abolitionism and Republicanism took strong footholds in the southern provinces. Thousands of slaves were freed by their owners in São Paulo and elsewhere in the south.[30]

The slaves themselves sensed the imminent approach of freedom and they began to desert the plantations. They fled to the cities where they placed themselves under the protection of the abolitionists, or else they fled to the interior of the country.[31] The slaveowners appealed to the government, requesting that the army be used to recapture the fugitives, but a letter from Marshal Deodoro, the spokesman for the Military Club of Rio de Janeiro, asked that the army not be called upon to recapture "the poor blacks, who are fleeing from slavery."[32] The slaveowners thus found themselves deprived of all support.[33] The clergy had long been using its influence in opposing slavery, and the report in *O Paiz* of Joaquim Nabuco's audience with Pope Leo XIII supported the church's opposition to slavery and encouraged Princess Isabel, who was regent in the absence of Dom Pedro II, to declare to the legislative house that "the extinction of the servile element has now become an aspiration of all classes in Brazil."[34] The condemnation of slavery in the press and from the orator's platform was almost unanimous. With the respectful but firm refusal of the army to capture the fleeing slaves, the law abolishing slavery in Brazil, which was passed by the House of Deputies

28. Martin, "Slavery and Abolition . . . ," p. 188.
29. *Contribuições*, p. 688.
30. Moraes, p. 864.
31. Duque-Estrada, p. 216; Galanti, V, 48.
32. Duque-Estrada, p. 216; *Contribuições*, p. 812.
33. Galanti, V, 49.
34. *Ibid.; Martin, "Slavery and Abolition . . . ,"* p. 191.

and approved by the Senate on May 13, 1888, was "no more than the recognition of a fact already existing."[35] The law of 1888 freed the slaves and in doing so provided no compensation for the great financial loss suffered by their owners. Dom Pedro, ill in Italy at the time, congratulated the Brazilian people and sent them his blessing.

The lofty level to which the abolition sentiment had ascended caused Isabel to neglect to mention indemnity to slaveowners for the loss of their property. The slaveowners themselves were reluctant to mention indemnity and those who had agitated for emancipation staunchly opposed any payment. Therefore the slaveowners, desiring an indemnity, yet refusing to demand one, blamed the dynasty. These powerful landowners, who had been supporters of the monarchy since 1822, were wounded financially and began to withdraw their support from the dynasty. Many of them simply withdrew from political life; others, particularly in the provinces of São Paulo, Minas Gerais, and Rio de Janeiro, turned to Republicanism. Their financial loss was indeed a heavy one. The value of the 720,000 slaves liberated on May 13, 1888, was estimated at some 485,225 *contos*, more than $200,000,000.[36]

Abolition as a factor of imperial disintegration has received considerable attention from the writers of Brazilian history, but the religious question was also a factor of profound significance when Dom Pedro II was forced to relinquish control of the government. The differences displayed by so many of the Conservatives showed that the conflict between the government and the church had aroused strong feelings of resentment.

The bitter conflict between the church and the state, which made the hierarchy of the church indifferent to the fate of the dynasty, had its roots in the distant past. Article five of the Constitution of Brazil stated that the Apostolic Roman Catholic religion would continue to be the religion of the state.[37] The statement including the words "would continue to be" indicated that Brazil was accepting the religion which it had inherited from Portugal, and that any laws which had restricted the action of the Catholic hierarchy during the colonial period would continue to restrict it during the period of independence. Thus, the *placet*, which regulated the publication and adherence to papal commands within Brazil, was a Portuguese

35. *Contribuições*, p. 812.
36. Percy Alvin Martin, "Causes of the Collapse of the Brazilian Empire," *Hispanic American Historical Review*, IV, 8; Duque-Estrada, p. 261.
37. Maria G. L. de Andrade, *História do Brasil* (Rio de Janerio, 1888), pp. 193-219; *Contribuições*, p. 496.

inheritance. Although the church could not officially recognize such a regulation, in practice it still made concessions, because the Constitution of Brazil recognized the clergy as a separate class closely allied with the organization of the government.

Only the most favorable circumstances would have permitted this tacit agreement between the two powers to endure indefinitely. The European revolutions of 1848, which were encouraged by the Masonic order, caused Pope Pius IX to renew his condemnation of that order. The lodges of the Masons in France and in Italy particularly aroused the ire of the Pope because of their anti-Catholic propaganda and their revolutionary tendencies. In Brazil, however, the Masons had expended most of their radical force during the independence movement. Their activity was mainly concerned with mutual aid, deeds of charity, and the encouragement of mild liberal aspirations by members of their organization.[38] Fortunately, too, the apostolic condemnations of the Masonic order were stated in such general terms that the clergy of Brazil were not required to interfere with the lodges of Brazil during the first half of the nineteenth century.[39]

The peace which existed between the church and the state probably could have continued until the end of the empire period in Brazil had it not been for the ultramontane tendencies of a Capuchin friar, Dom Vital Maria Gonçalves de Oliveira, who was installed as Bishop of Olinda on May 24, 1872. The new Bishop of Olinda was only twenty-eight years of age. He had been trained in France, where the Masonic lodges had played vital roles in revolutions during the nineteenth century and where the lodges were sponsors of demands for social change. It is possible that Dom Vital's experience with the French lodges influenced his action after he became Bishop of Olinda.[40] Some of the general anti-religious tendencies of the Masons seemed to be present in the Brazilian lodges. When the Council of State was hearing the case against the Bishop of Olinda in 1874, one of the members who opposed punishing the bishop, the Viscount of Abaete, said that he had once belonged to a lodge but had withdrawn from it almost forty years before 1874. In criticism of the lodges he said, "I never heard the word 'God' pronounced there. That sweet word is replaced by a circumlocution—Supreme Architect of the Universe."[41] More influential on the action of the

38. Calogeras, p. 236.
39. Pereira da Silva, *Memórias do meu tempo*, II, 155.
40. Viscount de Taunay, *O visconde de Rio Branco* (2nd ed.; São Paulo, 1930), p. 195; Fernando de Azevedo, *A cultura brasileira* (2nd ed.; São Paulo, 1944), p. 139.
41. *Contribuições*, p. 496.

Bishop of Olinda than the anti-religious tendencies of the lodges was the papal encyclical of 1864, which condemned Masonry, but which the imperial government would not permit to be enforced in Brazil.[42] The rigorous attitude of the new bishop was known to the lodges of Olinda and his presence was resented.[43] Before his arrival the Masons had formulated a plan of attack against him and he was greeted with an onslaught of bitter denunciations.

The new bishop did not immediately answer the attack of the Masons, but instead he began to institute quietly a series of reforms within his religious domain. When one of the local lodges announced its plans to celebrate a High Mass in celebration of its anniversary, he decided to oppose this move of a group, which in his opinion was an enemy of the Catholic church. In a restricted announcement he commanded that no member of the clergy take part in the celebration. The order was obeyed and the Mass was not held.

The Masons dominated the Soledade *irmandade*, a brotherhood both civil and ecclesiastical. As an act of reprisal, they elected as leader of the brotherhood Ayres Gama, who was not only an old and respected Mason but also editor of *Verdade*, a Masonic organ in whose pages the bishop had been insulted.[44] The bishop then sought the expulsion of all Masons from membership in the brotherhood. Not only did the Masons object to this attempt to exclude them, but others who were sympathetic toward the Masons also protested. These objections were taken to the president of the province. Meanwhile two priests who refused to adjure their connection with the Masonic order were suspended by the bishop, and the members of the brotherhood who refused to withdraw from the lodges were threatened with suspension.

Three times the *irmandade* of Soledade refused the command of the bishop to expel the Masons from the brotherhood, and on January 5, 1873, the *irmandade* was suspended. The members were prohibited from appearing as religious associates, from wearing religious habits, and from receiving new members. Certain restrictions would be removed when the members renounced Masonry or expelled the Masons. In order to avoid a conflict with the government, the bishop declared that the suspension "only referred to the religious or spiritual part of the *irmandades*."[45]

42. Lima, *O império brasileiro*, p. 167.
43. Calogeras, p. 238.
44. *Contribuições*, p. 480.
45. *Ibid.*; Lima, *O império brasileiro*, p. 168; Calogeras, p. 239.

On March 25, 1873, the Bishop of Pará, Dom Antonio de Macedo Costa, who also had been trained in France and who was the author of a book entitled *A Resistência dos bispos, as suspensões extrajudiciais e o recurso à corôa*, joined the Bishop of Olinda in his crusade against the Masonic order. In a pastoral letter to the members of his religious family, he announced that Masonry must be opposed because it was morally, religiously, and socially destructive to the good of the people.[46] His letter stated that "Only those Masons who declare in a written statement that they no longer belong to a lodge may continue to participate in brotherhoods."[47] Any brotherhood which refused this command would be suspended from all religious functions for the duration of its rebellion. Five brotherhoods were suspended in Pará because of their disobedience.

Rio Branco at this time was both leader of the government and grand master of the Masonic order. Most of the men who were in the higher government offices were members of the lodges. Dom Pedro himself had served for a time as an official in the order. The conflict which was about to begin found most of the men who were influential in the government allied to the Masonic order and to the supremacy of the state over the church.

The seriousness of the problem was recognized by the government and an effort was made to settle the conflict without official intervention. On February 15, 1873, a member of the cabinet, João Alfredo Corrêa de Oliveira, in a letter to the Bishop of Olinda, sought to avoid a church-state conflict. The minister pointed out that the government was concerned over the disturbances which the bishop's action had caused in the province, and he reminded the bishop that papal bulls which did not have the sanction of the government could not be enforced in Brazil.[48] In reply, the bishop reminded the minister of the public animosity displayed by the Masons at the time of his arrival, and added that had he been an old man with only a few years of service before him he could have been negligent of duty and perhaps been forgiven. But instead he was a young man with a very long time to serve.[49] The bishop revealed his attitude in unmistakable terms when he wrote:

I limit myself to saying concerning the absence of imperial sanction to the Papal Bull of 1865 that in a statement of September 25, 1865, the Holy Father formally condemned Masonry, even in countries

46. *Contribuições*, p. 481; Moraes, p. 398.
47. *Contribuições*, p. 481.
48. Pereira da Silva, *Memórias do meu Tempo*, II, 157.
49. *Contribuições*, p. 484; Taunay, p. 133.

where the secular power tolerates it. And that is enough for the Catholic.[50]

The government also sought to use the influence of Domingos Sanguigni, papal internuncio, and requested that he urge the bishop to modify his position. Sanguigni, however, while advising moderation to the bishop, at the same time offered suggestions on how the bishop might improve his position.[51] Dom Vital rejected Sanguigni's suggestions and appealed to Pope Pius IX for further authority in dealing with the brotherhoods. In response to Dom Vital's appeal, the Pope praised the zeal of the prelate and gave him authority to work vigorously against the Masons and the rebelling brotherhoods. However, he suspended the excommunications of the Masonic members of the brotherhoods for one year and permitted all who had been excommunicated to be allowed to absolve themselves during that year. He also ordered that the instructions given to the Bishop of Olinda be given to all of the bishops of Brazil so that they could take action against the Masons and the brotherhoods. This letter was published in all of the dioceses of Brazil on May 29, 1873.[52]

The appeals of the suspended brotherhoods were placed before the Council of State which, after studying the appeals, concluded that the bishops in their action against the brotherhoods had exceeded the limits of their authority.[53] The council reaffirmed the doctrine of imperial sanction of papal bulls and by a majority vote ordered that the bishops withdraw the interdicts within fifteen days or suffer the penalty of imprisonment.[54] The bishops refused to withdraw the interdicts and also refused to defend themselves before a civil court. On February 21, 1874, Dom Vital was sentenced to four years' imprisonment at hard labor, and on July 1, 1874, Dom Macedo Costa received a similar sentence. Dom Pedro II modified the sentences of the bishops and deleted the part condemning them to hard labor.[55]

While the trials of the bishops were in progress, the government, seeking to prevent the conflict with the church from reaching major proportions, sent an envoy to the Pope. The man selected for the mission was Baron Penedo, a competent lawyer and an experienced diplomat. Penedo was personally acquainted with Pope Pius IX and with the papal secretary of state, Cardinal Antonelli. He had met

50. Lima, *O império brasileiro*, p. 169.
51. *Contribuições*, p. 486.
52. *Ibid.*, p. 490; *Lima, O império brasileiro*, p. 170.
53. *Contribuições*, p. 495.
54. *Ibid.*; Taunay, p. 133.
55. Taunay, p. 134.

them while on a mission to the Holy See during 1858. The instructions given the envoy were in the opinion of one eminent Brazilian statesman, Joaquim Nabuco, ''an ultimatum, because the imprisonment of the bishops was like spiritual reprisals against the Pope.''[56] Nabuco regarded the Penedo mission as a provocation rather than an attempt to achieve peace with the church. The envoy's instructions were such as might arouse the ire of the Pope, since he was ordered to obtain a papal order instructing the bishops to obey the Constitution of Brazil. He was not to negotiate on the basis of individuals or companies, but the affair was to be negotiated as a matter of principle.[57] The baron was instructed to lay two choices before the Pope. Pius must either submit entirely to the will of the Brazilian government and order that the bishops resign themselves to the position of public employees, obedient to the orders of the imperial hierarchy, or else the government would encourage anti-Catholic movements in Brazil.[58] In a letter written by the Brazilian minister of foreign affairs on August 21, 1873, Penedo was urged to play down the anti-religious tendencies of the Masons. ''There are some,'' he wrote, ''who have a certain liberty of thought in matters of religion but generally speaking, the Masons are good Catholics.''[59]

Fortunately for the religious peace of Brazil, the baron, a skilled diplomat, realized that an attempt to adhere strictly to his instructions would intensify rather than mitigate the conflict between the church and the state. He used every effort to settle the conflict by gentle means and appealed to the Pope to end the conflict which was disturbing the country's religious peace. His statements to the papal secretary of state were indefinite, but they conveyed the idea that Brazil, while having constitutional means to punish the bishops and to end the conflict, preferred to have the Pope settle the matter.[60] These vague assurances led Pius to believe that the trial of the bishops would be dropped as soon as he assumed responsibility for settlement of the conflict.[61] The baron's statement was considered by a committee of cardinals and on December 20, 1873, Penedo sent the following message to the Brazilian foreign minister: ''the Holy Father is disposed to employ those means . . . he considers appropriate to end the deplorable conflict.'' He then informed the minister that

56. *Contribuições*, p. 507.
57. *Ibid.*
58. *Ibid.*, p. 508.
59. *Ibid.*
60. *Ibid.*, p. 509; Lima, *O império brasileiro*, p. 146.
61. *Contribuições*, p. 508; Calogeras, p. 242.

the Pope had ordered Cardinal Antonelli to write an official letter to the Bishop of Olinda. The bishop was to be censured and ordered to remove the interdicts upon the organizations within the diocese. "The Cardinal has shown the letter to me and I am authorized to inform your excellency that the tone of the letter is severe."[62] This letter was never published and the papal secretary refused to give the baron a copy.

Before the letter from the Pope could be published in Brazil, Pius learned of the imprisonment of the two bishops. Incensed at what was regarded as the betrayal of a promise, he revoked the letter and gave the rebelling clerics his full support. Cardinal Antonelli in a formal note explained that "If the Holy Father had imagined that the bishops would be imprisoned and condemned for following the rules of his sacred ministry, he would never have granted the courteous disposition."[63] The papal nuncio in Brazil on February 22, 1874, protested against the imprisonment of the bishops. In a statement which was delivered to the Brazilian foreign minister, he directed attention to the violation of ecclesiastical immunity in the case of the two bishops. The protest was deeply resented by the government officials since they regarded it as a criticism of the competency of the Supreme Tribunal of Justice by an official of a foreign government. The nuncio was informed that his protest was "impertinent and useless."[64]

Dom Pedro II had supported his ministers during the conflict with the church, and he is reported to have suggested that the bishops be imprisoned. The firm stand taken by the Emperor reinforced the ministers' action to force the bishops to obey the laws of the empire. The clergy were convinced that Dom Pedro had supported the position taken by his ministers, and in 1890, Dom Antonio de Macedo Costa, then primate of Brazil, wrote in a message to the members of his religious family that "the throne disappeared, . . . and the altar? The altar still stands."[65] Amnesty was granted to the two imprisoned bishops by Princess Isabel when she was regent during the absence of Dom Pedro in 1875.[66] The amnesty also included the cancellation of action which had been taken against other ecclesiastics involved in the conflict.[67] Soon after this amnesty an order from the Pope ended the

62. *Contribuições*, p. 510; *Pereira de Silva, Memórias do meu tempo*, II, 160.
63. *Contribuições*, p. 512.
64. *Ibid.*, p. 523.
65. *Ibid.*, p. 528; Lima, *O império brasileiro*, p. 179.
66. Moraes, p. 404.
67. Pereira da Silva, *Memórias do meu tempo*, II, 172.

interdicts against the brotherhoods; however, the order condemned the infiltration of Masons into the religious brotherhoods and into the private spiritual domain of the church.[68]

Republicanism was a third factor of major importance in contributing to the fall of Dom Pedro II. The monarchy had been originally intended by many Brazilians as only a temporary form of government, but José Bonifácio de Andrade, a sincere monarchist, had been able to cement the arrangement into a permanent one. The declaration of the majority of Dom Pedro II had ended republican agitation during the period from 1840 to 1868. But the years following the Paraguayan War were exceedingly favorable for the development of the republican ideal. The lines which in other years had distinguished the Liberal from the Conservative disappeared. The program which the Liberal party had advanced in the late 1860's had been adopted and partially passed by the Conservative party. This move deprived the Liberals of a program, and since they could not adopt the position which the Conservatives had held, they were forced to devise a program along more radical lines. The new tactics of the Conservatives, who had been aided in their rise to power by the Emperor, caused many of the thinking men among the Liberals of Brazil to feel that the monarchy had fulfilled its mission and that Brazil should now be more closely identified with the other nations of the American continents, all of whom were republics.[69]

The men who had signed the Republican Manifesto in 1871 did not expect that the publication of the manifesto would cause the immediate fall of the empire. Its publication was intended to be a signal or a call to unite the forces of opposition to the monarchy. Without the existence of an organized party the republican ideal could not have been effective. Joaquim Nabuco in a letter to his son said that the formation of the Republican party was "a great misfortune for the Liberal party, which each day is becoming more disorganized."[70]

The publication of the manifesto did succeed in uniting the forces opposed to monarchy. Republican clubs and journals were organized in many of the provinces of Brazil. On January 17, 1872, a Republican group was organized in São Paulo at the home of Dr. Americo Brasiliense. A committee composed of Brasiliense, Campos Salles, and Americo de Campos was named to invite friends to become a

68. Lima, *O império brasileiro*, p. 180.
69. Mattoso, p. 11.
70. *Contribuições*, p. 564.

nucleus for the Republican party of São Paulo. The Republicans of São Paulo, who believed in federal principles and local autonomy, agreed that each club would retain its independence and liberty of action. News of the formation of the Republican party of São Paulo was published in the *Correio Paulistano* on March 19, 1872. The committee which had been formed to promote the organization of Republican clubs in the province was careful to emphasize the peaceful intention of the new party and to deny accusations that the party desired a violent solution to the slavery question. In a circular dated January 18, 1872, the Republicans declared that the flag under which they fought was "moderation, peace and legality."[71]

The Republican Congress which met in Itu on April 18, 1873, had originally been scheduled for December 25, 1872, but had been delayed until the opening of the Ituana railway, which permitted more people to attend. Representatives were present from seventeen towns, indicating that the growth of the idea in the province had been rapid. The congress held another session on July 1, 1873, attended by representatives from twenty-seven towns. At this congress a commission was elected to direct the party during the period when the congress was not in session. It was agreed also that this commission would study and formulate a political organization for the province on the basis of municipal and provincial autonomy. The commission met several times and on October 19, 1873, signed a project which was a federal constitution for the province of São Paulo. It was the first Brazilian state constitution, although sixteen years had to pass and the monarchy to fall before it could receive serious consideration.[72]

The Paulista Republicans in 1873 were indefinite in their policies regarding abolition. They promised that should they rise to power, they would free the slaves more or less slowly, not uniformly through the country, but as fast as they could be replaced by free labor. Owners of freed slaves were to receive an indemnity. The Republicans also sought to quiet the fears of the Conservatives by declaring that their movement was a peaceful one, seeking "only the conquest of public opinion."[73]

A decline in interest in the party was noted in 1875, the year during which a Republican press was destroyed by the police of Rio de Janeiro. Only twenty-four delegates appeared at the São

71. *Ibid.*
72. *Ibid.*, p. 566.
73. *Ibid.*, p. 569.

Paulo Republican Congress for that year, although many more had been elected and authorized to attend. The congress of 1875 approved the suggested basic constitution, authorized the founding of a journal as a party organ, and named a commission to publish a manifesto on the position of the party in relation to the religious question. The manifesto, which was published on April 8, 1875, attacked the position of the church and demanded: (1) full religious freedom and equality of all before the civil and political authority, (2) abolition of the official character of the Catholic church and its separation from the civil power and the suppression of all privileges of the church, (3) separation of religious and secular education, (4) civil marriage, (5) civil registration of births and deaths, and (6) secularization of the cemeteries and administration of them by the towns and cities.[74] During the years 1875 to 1877 there were no meetings of the Republican Congress, but the permanent commission remained active. It devoted its efforts to increasing the number of Republican voters and in 1878 the party obtained the majority of votes in some towns. In the election to the House of Deputies, Americo Brasiliense obtained only thirty-five votes less than the winning candidate.

São Paulo was the only province in which the Republican party was completely organized during the years before 1880. In the other provinces during the decade 1870-1880, Republicans limited themselves to propaganda, the publication of journals, and the formation of clubs. In Minas, despite the adhesion to the Republican Manifesto by a large number of *fazendeiros*, the movement lacked the stability of the Paulista organization.

Republican clubs and journals appeared in other provinces. A journal called *A Democracia* was founded in Rio Grande do Sul in 1872. A Republican club was organized in Recife in December, 1871, with José Maria de Albuquerque Mello as president. Several Republican journals quickly sprang up and vanished in Pernambuco in the 1870's: *A República Federativa* which appeared only a few times, and which was the organ of the *Clube Republicano* of that province; *O Seis de Março*, which was published from March 6 to June 12, 1872; *O Pernambucano*, whose first number appeared on April 20, 1872; *A Luz*, whose first number appeared on April 9, 1873; and the bi-weekly, *O Republicano Federativo*, which appeared on July 15, 1874, and ceased publication on December 4, 1876.[75] In the provinces of the extreme north, Republicanism seemed limited to the formation of clubs and the publication of short-lived journals.

74. *Ibid.*, p. 573.
75. *Ibid.*, p. 574.

In Amazonas, *O Augus* appeared from April 8, 1870, to June 30, 1872. In Pará, *O Tira-Dentes*, edited by Julio Cesar Ribeiro de Sousa, was published on February 14, 1871. *O Futuro*, which appeared in 1872, published only one number, and its founder, Dr. Joaquim José de Assis, returned to the ranks of the monarchists in 1876. *A Província do Pará* was the only Republican journal of the north which was long-lived; it ceased publication as late as 1908. Only one Republican journal was published in Maranhão during the 1870's, and when its editor, Dr. Antonio de Almeida Oliveira went to reside in Rio de Janeiro, he joined the Liberal party and was elected to the House of Deputies and later became a minister of state. He explained his Republicanism to his new colleagues as "dreams of youth."[76]

When the Liberal party rose to power in 1878, Dom Pedro, who no longer regarded the Republicans with indifference, suggested that a Republican of high intellectual standards be included in the new ministry.[77] He hoped in this manner to neutralize the efforts of the propaganda of the party. This imperial tactic did have an influence upon the development of the party, which in many of the provinces was not well organized. In São Paulo, where the party had greatest stability, its leaders quickly saw the strategy behind the imperial move and took steps to forestall a stampede from Republican ranks. Campos Salles said that the situation created by the Liberals' inclusion of a Republican in their government was a test of the sincerity and firmness of the Republicans. A signer of the Republican Manifesto of 1870, Lafayette Rodrigues Pereira, finally accepted the office of minister of justice in the Liberal ministry. In the opinion of Sinimbu, who organized the ministry, this move "deprived the Republicans of too valuable an element."[78] Republican journals, following the advice of party leaders, warned Republicans "to remain at their posts of battle."[79] The *Gazeta de Campinas* on January 11, 1878, a few days after the organization of the new ministry, warned that "the duty of the Republican party is to know how to guard firmly its positions in order to act with decision and efficiency, no matter what the turn of events may be."[80]

During 1878 the Republicans of São Paulo caused the assembly of that province to present a law which forbade the entrance of slaves into the province. Though the president of the province refused

76. *Ibid.*, p. 576.
77. Hornane Tavares de Sá, *The Brasilians, People of Tomorrow* (New York, 1917), p. 171.
78. *Contribuições*, p. 576.
79. *Ibid.*, p. 577.
80. *Ibid.*

to sanction this project, it was revived in following sessions until 1881 when it was made a law. In the elections of October 31, 1881, Campos Salles, Republican candidate and a future president of the Republic of Brazil, was defeated in the election for deputy by only seven votes. Three years later, on December 1, 1884, three men who proclaimed their opposition to the monarchy were elected to the House of Deputies: Prudente de Moraes, another future president of the republic, Campos Salles, and Alvaro Botelho. The first two were elected by the voters of São Paulo and the third deputy was elected by the voters of Minas Gerais. Prudente de Moraes, once in the House of Deputies, made a profession of his political faith. He stated frankly that he was a Republican: "My political program is in the Manifesto of December 3, 1871, which all of the country knows. My purpose is the substitution of the monarchy by a federative republic." He then stated that the Republicans for the present would only accept and support the acts of the government "which conform with the true interests of society and only support reforms which sustain democratic ideas.."[81]

These three Republicans were the only members of their party to reach the House of Deputies until the last year of the imperial regime. The members of the Liberal and Conservative parties became alarmed and joined forces to prevent the election of Republican deputies to the House.[82]

With the exception of São Paulo, Republicanism, after arousing wide interest during the 1870's, languished in other Brazilian provinces where many of the early converts returned to their original parties.[83] However, the emancipation of the slaves provided the opportunity for which the Republican leaders had been waiting. The conflict with the church, which decreased the interest of that religious body in the perpetuation of the imperial regime, and the infiltration of Republicanism into the ranks of the army, which intensified the conflict then being waged between the generals and the government officials, deprived the throne of two of its chief supports. The one remaining support was lost when the slaves were freed without indemnity to their owners; the resultant Republican effort made 1888 the turning point in the history of the Brazilian Republican party.[84]

81. Galanti, V, 95.
82. *Ibid.*
83. Pereira da Silva, *Memórias do meu tempo*, II, 173.
84. Calmon, *História Social* . . . , II, 370; Martin, ''Causes of the Collapse . . . ,'' p. 17.

Chapter Five

Marshal Deodoro, Defender of the Military Class

Soon after Deodoro had sent the telegram in which he supported the protest made by Lieutenant Colonel Senna Madureira, some of the officers of the Porto Alegre garrison asked the president of the province and commandant of arms for permission to discuss the Madureira protest. After granting permission for the meeting, Deodoro informed the officers: "Be it known that I am already firing from our advance posts!"[1] The Republicans of Rio Grande do Sul, seizing the opportunity created by the schism between the military and the government in that province, immediately identified themselves with the disgruntled military. An editorial entitled "Together with Honor" in A Federação on September 28, 1886, praised the stand which the marshal had made in defense of the dignity and legitimate rights of the army.[2]

News of the meetings and discussions of the case of Lieutenant Colonel Madureira and the extremely critical attitude of the officers was reported in the newspapers of Rio de Janeiro. Baron Cotegipe, president of the ministry, noting the adverse effect of these reports in the capital, asked the marshal to give an explanation for the conduct of the officers. When informed that "the meeting resulted from the just and general sentiment of a deeply offended army" and that the meetings had the approval and consent of the marshal, Cotegipe pointed out to Deodoro the great responsibility with which the government had intrusted him. In terms fashioned so as not to arouse the ire of the marshal, Cotegipe said that it was not wise to authorize meetings which could attain unforeseen consequences. "I recommend that you as president of the province use your authority and influence in order to end the agitation."[3] Cotegipe asked that detailed information about the protest meetings be sent to the government.

1. Fonseca Filho, p. 30; Senna, p. 251.
2. Fonseca Filho, p. 31.
3. Anfriso Fialho, p. 65.

The reply which Marshal Deodoro sent to the president of the ministry indicated that the conflict between the government and the officers should be settled at once. Deodoro boldly placed himself at the head of the resistance to the ministerial *avisos*. "All officers, generals and others, including myself, with good reason are showing concern for the new and vexing imposition which deprives us of prompt and immediate defense."[4] The marshal considered that the prohibition against answering the attack of the foes of the military class was "hard, humiliating and prejudiced against the interests of the army." In his opinion the *avisos* were an imposition by means of which the enemies of the army sought to persecute it. Answering Cotegipe's reference to his duty as president of the province and commandant of the army, he bitterly stated: "If I have duties as president of this province and commander of the army, I also have duties as a soldier who is offended by the ingratitude shown the military class."[5] The effects of the sharply worded message were mitigated by the minister's being informed that Deodoro, as spokesman for the military of Rio Grande do Sul, asked the aid of the minister in securing justice for the military class.

Cotegipe, cognizant of the seriousness of the situation and flattered by the appeal which the marshal made to him, placed the matter of the legality of the ministerial *avisos* before the Supreme Military Council. This council was a judicial body for matters relating to the armed forces, and its personnel consisted almost entirely of retired, high-ranking military and naval officers. After having informed Deodoro of this action, the minister expressed the desire that all meetings of the officers of the province be prohibited and that order be restored and maintained. The marshal expressed satisfaction with this settlement of the question, but the proud old soldier did not think that Cotegipe was fully aware of the degree of his resentment of the doctrine of administrative *avisos*, and on October 6, 1886, he sent the following letter to him:

The aviso of the Minister of War of September 4, 1884, in which that minister reprimanded Lieutenant Colonel Madureira, disgusted the military deeply. I am united with them by honor and by military duty and if I did not take the initiative in the matter it was because the positions which the imperial government honors me require that I transmit to the government the just complaints of those who are under my administration. Had I taken an integral part in the meet-

4. *Ibid.*
5. *Ibid.*, p. 66.

ings my presence would have given the meetings an official aspect, thus causing the spontaneity of the class to vanish from it.[6]

Realizing that Deodoro had not altered his position, Cotegipe, after consultation with the cabinet, dismissed the marshal from the office of acting president of Rio Grande do Sul. In doing so he pointed out to the marshal the absence of discipline in the armed forces of the province. An army which protested against the acts of the minister of war, the first military authority in the empire, in time might protest against the acts of the government itself: "We shall have then, a deliberating army, one which is incompatible with the civil liberty of the nation."[7]

It may be recalled that Cotegipe had hoped that Deodoro would become the "Caxias" of the party, and he had predicted that certain honors would fall to him because of his being the military leader of the Conservative party. Deodoro's firm position as defender of his class rather than defender of a party led the president of the ministry to remark in his letter of dismissal that "The cabinet and I regret that your excellency, in whom we have placed greater confidence than in any other officer, has raised such serious obstructions."[8] Still seeking to retain some working understanding with the general, Cotegipe urged him to co-operate with the new president of the province and to do all that he could to end the agitation in Rio Grande do Sul.

Marshal Deodoro has been described as "loyal as steel, rash to the point of temerity."[9] In replying to Cotegipe's letter of dismissal, he bitterly denounced the policies of the government in a statement which came close to being a declaration of war upon the government:

The theme in question is undisciplined, tumultuous, seditious meetings on the part of the military. There have been motives for tumultuous meetings, because the military can not and should not be subjected to offenses and insults from the Francos de Sá and Simplicios whose immunity is not authority to give insults, nor does it exempt them from a necessary and suitable response.[10]

Advancing from the specific to the general, Marshal Deodoro made the names of the two hated civilians plural so that the president of the ministry could observe that the anger of the army was directed

6. *Ibid.*, p. 67
7. *Ibid.*
8. Antonio Joaquim Ribas, *Perfil biográfico de Campos Salles* (Rio de Janeiro, 1896), p. 110; Fialho, p. 67.
9. Calogeras, p. 263.
10. Fialho, p. 68.

at all of the *casacas* (name derived from the long, black, Prince Albert coat which was required dress for politicians) who were seeking to curtail the pride and honor of the military class. He accused the government of not only giving consideration to the civilian offenders but also of giving further offense by publicly reprimanding the two officers. An old servant of the government, a distinguished, correct, and decent officer, had been shamed before the world in order that satisfaction be given to a man who had no authority over him. Expressing the sentiments of his class, the marshal wrote:

The wound was painful, cruel and mortal and it bled with good reason while Madureira and Cunha Matos were under the pressure of the injustices of which they were victims. . . . If fate decides the decline of the military class, on the day that I, despairing that I cannot be superior to a commander of the national guard, a simple and special political figure, on that day, I shall break my sword and ashamed, seek as a means of livelihood, after the example of many others, the chair of deputy, so that I too may insult whom I wish.[11]

On receipt of this denunciation of the government's policies, Cotegipe immediately informed Deodoro that the differences in attitude between the government and its trusted agent could not endure without prejudicing the interests of the state. He ordered Deodoro to report for duty at an office which he would occupy in Rio de Janeiro. Fearing the possibility of an armed rebellion in Rio Grande do Sul, the minister ordered the transfer of all of the officers who had been active in the protest meetings. Lieutenant Colonel Madureira, Colonel José Simião de Oliveira, the director of the provincial military school and a devoted friend of General Viscount Pelotas, and Colonel Bernardo Vasques were all ordered to report to the minister of war for assignment to new duties.

Later the marshal was to be criticized by Cotegipe in 1887 and by Cunha Mattos after the establishment of the republic because of his opposition to the use of the ministerial *aviso*. Cotegipe stated in the Senate that Deodoro had used the *aviso* with more rigor than the minister of war against an officer who had criticized him in the press while he was commandant of arms in Rio Grande do Sul. Cunha Mattos in an article published in the *Jornal do Comércio* asserted that Deodoro's break with the ministry was caused by ministerial interference in the transfer of an officer. The transferred officer, a friend of Silveira Martins, had secured the latter's inter-

11. Galanti, V, 99. The Cotegipe-Deodoro correspondence reprinted from the *Diário Oficial*, May 8, 1891, is found in Fleiuss, *História administrativa* . . . , pp. 413-418.

vention and instead of being transferred to a distant post, he was ordered to report to Rio de Janeiro. This incident occurred while the Senna Madureira case was developing.[12] While these occurrences throw some light on the cause of the marshal's intense hatred for Silveria Martins, the basis of his opposition to the ministry seems to have been that of the soldier who resented the assaults by the despised *casacas* upon the honor and pride of the military class. Still another explanation offered for the marshal's hatred of Silveira Martins was the rumor that the two had clashed over the affection of a pretty woman.[13]

Deodoro's opposition to the ministry was known at all of the military posts of the empire, and the government took steps to prevent the military from celebrating the arrival of the marshal in Rio de Janeiro. Field Marshal Severiano da Fonseca, an older brother of Deodoro, was the commandant of the Military School of Rio de Janeiro, and the ministry ordered that he prevent the students of that school from leaving the campus on the day of Deodoro's arrival. However, the students of the school, disobeying the order of their commandant, greeted Deodoro's arrival at the place of embarkation with cheers. Severiano da Fonseca, having failed to carry out the order of the ministry, submitted his resignation as commandant of the school. The ministry, realizing that the field marshal had executed the order but had not been obeyed, refused to accept his resignation.

On November 3, 1886, the question of the legality of the *avisos* of the minister of war which had been submitted to the Supreme Military Council was settled by an imperial resolution which decreed that "According to the Constitution, officers, like any other citizens, have the right to manifest their opinions through the use of the newspapers."[14] The council ruled that discussion of military or political issues in the newspapers between officers of the armed forces could not be permitted because of reasons of security. The decree was supported by popular opinion and was joyously welcomed by Republicans and abolitionists, who by this time were staunch supporters of the military class. Since the cases of Cunha Mattos and Senna Madureira involved discussion between military and civilians, the *avisos* had been unjustly used against the two

12. Monteiro, *Pesquisas e depoimentos* . . . , p. 133; Rocha Pombo, X, 58.
13. Madeiro E. Albuqurque, *Quando eu era viva . . . Memórias, 1867 a 1934* (Porto Alegre, 1942), p. 83.
14. Fialho, p. 72.

officers. It is possible that the conflict between the *casacas* and the military would have subsided had the ministry, in view of the decision of the Supreme Military Council and the imperial resolution supporting that decision, canceled the censures against the two officers.[15]

The politicians who controlled the government had expected to be supported by the decision of the Supreme Military Council. The fact that the council had been composed of retired military and naval officers had not prevented the government from placing the question before it. Cotegipe later said that this was done so that it could not be said that "civilians do not understand military legislation."[16] The question could have been submitted to the Council of State, or Lieutenant Colonel Madureira could have been granted the court-martial which he had demanded. The resolution giving the military the status of "citizens in uniforms" having been decreed, the ministry was reluctant to acknowledge its error by rescinding the censures against the two officers. It announced that the censures would be rescinded upon request of the two officers,[17] but Cunha Mattos and Senna Madureira refused to do this. Since the *avisos* used against them had been declared unconstitutional, they demanded that they be revoked by the minister of war.[18]

This attitude on the part of the ministry irritated the military and increased their opposition to the policies of the government. When Deodoro arrived in Rio de Janeiro this increased opposition and irritation was reflected in his failure to report to the minister of war for duty. Despite this breach of discipline the marshal was appointed quartermaster general of the army, an office which was reserved for high-ranking and respected soldiers. Deodoro was insulted further when Silveira Martins, speaking before the Senate, made vicious accusations against the marshal, declared that he had been guilty of abuse of authority while serving as president of Rio Grande do Sul, and that instead of being made quartermaster general, he should be tried before the Supreme Tribunal Justice. Marshal Deodoro was defended by Baron Lucena, the man whom Cotegipe had advised to become a friend of Deodoro so that the marshal might become "our Caxias."

During December, 1886, and January, 1887, a distinctly revolu-

15. *Jornal do Comércio* (Sept. 7, 1922), p. 400.
16. Monteiro, *Pesquisas e depoimentos* . . . , p. 138.
17. Ottoni, p. 86.
18. *Ibid.*, p. 87; Monteiro, *Pesquisas e depoimentos* . . . , p. 140.

tionary current was present in Rio de Janeiro. Abolitionists and Republicans echoed the demands of the military that the ministry revoke the censures against the two officers. Deodoro, who continued to be the strong man around whom the military and their sympathizers rallied, announced that a meeting of the officers of the Rio de Janeiro garrison would be held in the Recreio Dramático on February 2, 1887.[19] This was a bold assault upon the position of the ministry. During the long years of Dom Pedro's reign no such audacious act had occurred. The meeting was called for the expressed purpose of considering certain acts of the government. About two hundred officers were present at the gathering, and civilian sympathizers of the military filled the galleries of the theater. The arrival of the marshal caused tumultuous applause from the officers and the civilians.[20] Sharing the stage with Marshal Deodoro were Cunha Mattos and Senna Madureira, the two offended officers; Benjamin Constant, a professor of mathematics at the Military School and leader of the positivist movement in Brazil; and José Simeão, one of the instigators of the Rio Grande do Sul affair.

The following motion was presented and approved without discussion: "The army and naval officers present at this meeting do not consider the conflict between them and the government honorably ended for the military class while the unconstitutional *avisos*, which were justly condemned by the imperial resolution of last November 3, remain in effect."[21] The officers also agreed that only the ending of any attempt to punish those who had played a part in the military question would end the disgust which the army felt for the ministry. They appealed to Dom Pedro II to use his influence to end the agitation over the question. They gave full powers to Marshal Deodoro to represent them before the imperial government "with the intention of obtaining a final solution to the conflict which would be worthy of the imperial government and of the honor of the military class."[22]

Three days later, the *Jornal do Comércio*, alarmed at the tenor of the meeting, editorially asked:

What does the direct recourse to the sovereign signify? The only constitutional attribution applicable to the case being that of naming and dismissing freely the ministers, the recourse implicitly contained the request for the removal of the minister of war, or all of the cab-

19. *Jornal do Comércio* (Sept. 7, 1922), p. 400.
20. Monteiro, *Pesquisas e depoimentos* . . . , p. 137.
21. *Ibid.*
22. *Ibid.*, p. 138; *Jornal do Comércio* (Sept. 7, 1922), p. 400.

inet. Could this mean that these officers have united with the intent to use pressure and coercion?[23]

On the same day that this editorial appeared, Deodoro addressed his first letter to the Emperor. In the letter the marshal stated that he spoke for the army and all the military class. He asked if the Emperor knew of the injustices which had been inflicted upon the military, and he reviewed the events surrounding the cases of Cunha Mattos and Senna Madureira. Deodoro reminded the Emperor that the imperial resolution of November 3, 1886, had been disregarded by the ministry. Since that time no effort had been made to correct the injustice which had been done to the two officers. The marshal asked "in the name of the army, in the name of the military class, I beg Your Majesty to attend to the question and decide it with that complete justice which characterizes all of the acts of Your Imperial Majesty."[24] Deodoro's adjutant delivered the massage to the Emperor, who, after reading it, remarked that he would have to make a decision concerning the matter. The decision was made within a few hours. Marshal Deodoro was dismissed from the office of quartermaster general on the same day that the Emperor received the letter. It was announced later that the dismissal had followed a meeting of the Council of Ministers and that Dom Pedro II himself had presided.

It is possible that this move was intended to humiliate the proud marshal and force him to retire from the army. Anfriso Fialho, a contemporary, reports that he had warned the marshal that dismissal from the post of quartermaster general might be the answer the monarch would give to his letter. Referring to the possibility of his resigning from the army under such conditions, Deodoro said: "Never! I shall go where they order. I have no children and my wife is like a soldier."[25]

Instead of resigning in disgust, the marshal wrote a second letter to Dom Pedro on February 12, 1887. The Emperor was informed that the military asked only that an injustice be righted. Not only the military but the people understood the injustice of the government's procedure and their sympathy was with the army:

The matter is very serious, Senhor, and only one who knows nothing of valor and the fine points of honor or does not know of the possible consequences, could unmindfully face the torment which approaches.

23. *Jornal do Comércio* (Sept. 7, 1922), p. 400.
24. Fialho, p. 76
25. *Ibid.*

Senhor, your ministry deceives you! At least in this case. It has exasperated the army and provoked a reaction. . . . I await justice from Your Majesty, that justice which your minister of war has denied us. . . . On being denied the justice for which I beg, I shall be ashamed of the uniform which I wear.[26]

Soon after receiving this letter the Emperor accepted the resignation of the minister of war who had advocated drastic measures of reprisal against the military. The minister, Alfredo Chaves, had proposed that Deodoro be retired from the service and that certain of the military schools be closed. Cotegipe, referring to his dismissal at a later time, said, "It is all very well to advise 'punish, imprison, cut off heads,' but in practice many times we see ourselves obliged to moderate in order not to sacrifice higher interests."[27]

The tension between the government and the military was not relieved by this move because the new minister of war, Ribeiro Luz, did not revoke the censures. Agitation, encouraged by Republicans, abolitionists, and Liberals, increased during the spring of 1887. Still the ministry did not yield to the demands of the military. Deodoro remained the center of gravitation of the military question. As the time for the opening of Parliament approached, unrest was prevalent among the military in all of the provinces of Brazil.[28]

Deodoro decided to await the arrival of General Viscount Pelotas, who was a member of the Imperial Senate. Meanwhile Republicans, led by Quintino Bocayuva, sought to attach themselves to the military. Republican leaders from São Paulo, led by Campos Salles, came to the capital to confer with their cohorts in the home of Aristides Lobo about the plausibility of contacting Pelotas concerning the proclamation of the republic as a result of the military movement which seemed imminent. The Republican Serzedello got in touch with the general, pointing out to him the condition of Dom Pedro's health and suggesting that the time was opportune to proclaim the republic. However, Pelotas was not enthusiastic about the matter and deferred it by saying: "That will come later; for the present it is necessary to have the agreement of all the comrades."[29]

A few days after his interview with Serzedello, Pelotas conferred with Deodoro, Benjamin Constant and his brother Marciano de Magalhães, and Madureira. Present also were Serzedello, as repre-

26. *Ibid.*
27. Monteiro, *Pesquisas e depoímentos* . . . , p. 141.
28. Dr. Francisco José da Silveira Lobo, "Ultimo dias do monarquia em São Paulo," *Revista do Instituto Histórico e Geográfico de São Paulo*, XXVII, 123; Affonso de Carvalho, p. 353; Vianna, "A queda do império," p. 861.
29. Monteiro, *Pesquisas e depoímentos* . . . , p. 145.

sentative of the Military School, and an officer from each of the corps of the Rio de Janeiro garrison. It was proposed that the troops be sent into the streets to overthrow the government, since Dom Pedro, old and ill, was no longer in control. After a period of silence Pelotas turned to Marshal Deodoro and asked, "My comrade, what do you think of it?" Deodoro's reply to this question was "If it has to be tomorrow, or be it today, I am ready."[30]

After discussing the leadership of the troops and agreeing that Deodoro and himself would have joint command, Pelotas decided that an appeal signed by both of them should first be made to Parliament to settle the conflict peacefully. The appeal, actually an ultimatum, was published on May 14, 1887, reportedly before Deodoro had signed it. When the manifesto was brought to Deodoro for his signature, the marshal was conferring with Baron Lucena and without reading it he directed that it be published and promised to sign it the following day.[31] The manifesto reviewed the grievances of the military and concluded by stating that there was no other recourse for the military except an appeal to the nation, which from the beginning had given its support. This last protest, the manifesto stated, was made to Parliament because the military proposed to maintain its resistance to the constitutional censures until they received full satisfaction.[32]

Cotegipe continued to oppose revocation of the censures even after the publication of the manifesto. He declared that the censures would remain in effect until the officers requested that they be revoked, or until a minister of war revoked them of his own accord. His secret agents having informed him that Deodoro and Pelotas were planning a revolution, Cotegipe sought out Baron Lucena and requested that he go to Deodoro and seek to calm him.[33] The baron, who had continued his friendship with the military leader, accepted this mission only on condition that he not be required to report anything which would be detrimental to the interests of Deodoro. This provision was not needed, for the marshal made no secret of the plans of the military. During the interview with the baron he went to a desk in the room, opened a drawer, and drew from it a bundle of papers. The papers were pledges of support from all of the military garrisons of the provinces of Brazil with the exception of the garrison at Pernambuco.[34] The

30. *Ibid.*
31. Rocha Pombo, X, 67; Duque-Estrada, pp. 205-209.
32. Galanti, V, 191; Monteiro, *Pesquisas e depoimentos* . . . , p. 149.
33. Ottoni, p. 87.
34. Monteiro, *Pesquisas e depoimentos* . . . , p. 151; Rocha Pombo, X, 67; Vianna, "A queda do império," p. 861; Ottoni, p. 87.

fate of the empire lay in the hands of Marshal Deodoro because the garrisons placed themselves at his orders and gave him full power to act as he saw fit. With these papers in his hands Deodoro told Lucena that he would like him to inform the president of the ministry of all that he had seen and heard during their discussion. The marshal was so confident of his mastery of the situation that he informed Lucena that within a short time the ministry would fall, but that Cotegipe need not fear for his life because Deodoro guaranteed that he would not be harmed.[35]

On May 18, 1887, Cotegipe arose in the Senate and explained before that assembly the motives for the government's procedure in the cases of the two offended officers. The minister was relentless in his demands that the officers request that the censures be revoked, because in his opinion he was following a procedure which prevailed in all branches of government. "Military regulations state that an illegal order given by a superior to an inferior must be obeyed. Action may be taken against the superior after the illegal order has been obeyed." The president of the ministry then asked, "Cannot an order of the government, given by the authority of a law well or poorly understood, be, in similar circumstances, an order of a superior to an inferior?" Cotegipe also questioned in what way an injustice done to one member of the army could affect all of the military class.[36]

Pelotas, assuming full responsibility for the manifesto which he and Deodoro had signed, rebuffed Cotegipe's conciliatory speech and said that he was willing to discard his immunity as a senator and to face a Council of War to account for his publication of the manifesto. The concluding portion of his speech was a warning to the government:

The noble President of the Council knows well that it was a revolution which caused Dom Pedro I to abdicate; today the fact is accepted. I entreat the President of the Council to reconsider his act for love of this country, not for my own satisfaction, which is of little value: Solve this question in an honorable and dignified manner. If this is not done, we do not know what can happen tomorrow, despite the noble president's confidence in the armed forces which he has at his disposition. Such are the circumstances that it is easily possible that they fail him. Noble president reconsider . . . for love of this country, and who knows, but for love of its institutions.[37]

35. Rocha Pombo, X, 67.
36. *Ibid.*
37. Lima, *O império Brasileiro*, p. 163; Vianna, "A queda do império," p. 862; Rocha Pombo, X, 68.

Cotegipe eloquently and firmly defended the government's position. "I am able to reply to the noble senator and say to him that the government is in its place and the noble senator is not in his."[38] He sought to sway the general by an appeal to his past career as a soldier and a citizen of the empire.

Although the Liberal party was delighted to see the Conservatives embarrassed by this crisis, many of them who had encouraged the military were now fearful of the possibilities of the outcome of the situation. The staid *Jornal do Comércio* on May 19, 1886, warned that "enemies of the situation and of the sworn institutions are taking advantage of it with the risk of making all government impossible. No, a thousand times no!"[39] Saraiva, Liberal leader and a former president of the cabinet, who had not participated in the conflict between the government and the military, requested that the ministry seek a solution for the crisis which threatened the country. Silveira Martins and Affonso Celso, future Viscount Ouro Preto, offered to mediate between the military and the ministers. Cotegipe accepted their mediation and the two Liberals sought out Pelotas at his hotel.

In conjunction with the general they first considered the idea of a law giving retroactive effect to the imperial resolution of November 3, 1886. Reflection on this procedure convinced them that too much time would be consumed in passing a law.[40] It was then decided that the government should make the move at the request of the Senate. Cotegipe accepted the solution and called Ouro Preto's attention to an editorial in *O Paiz*, a Republican newspaper, which attacked the party system and parliamentarianism. Cotegipe said that "It is natural that it is unhappy and already because of its foresight it attacks parties and parliamentarianism. The reason is clear: the opportunity to embark the Republic in the waters of revolution is lost."[41]

Fearing the fall of his ministry because of the impending Senate resolution, Cotegipe sought to prepare João Alfredo to replace him as president of the ministry. However, João Alfredo did not wish to accept because of the threatening situation and because he did not wish the ministry to fall before the pressure of the military. He assured Cotegipe that he would solve the question and that he would

38. Monteiro, *Pesquisas e depoimentos* . . . , p. 153; Rocha Pombo, X, 68.
39. *Jornal do Comércio* (Sept. 7, 1922), p. 401.
40. Ouro Preto, "Advento da dictadura militar do Brasil," *RIHGB*, CL, 145.
41. Monteiro, *Pesquisas e depoimentos* . . . , p. 155; Rocha Pombo, X, 69.

receive the support of both parties. At a meeting of the ministers on the night of May 18, four members voted for the resignation of the ministry and two voted for its continuance. It was decided that the Senate should hold a secret session to consider the proposed solution of the crisis. However, João Alfredo urged that this step not be taken since such a move would cause public unrest and give the situation greater significance than it merited. In his opinion the question could be solved peacefully. Should the Senate accept the suggestion of the ministry, the public would consider the resolution as a censure of the ministry. He added that justice was on the side of the censured officers, since they suffered a punishment which an imperial resolution had declared unconstitutional. "The case was one of simple formality, since the government had declared that it would cancel the censures if the officers requested that they be cancelled."[42] It was revealed later that João Alfredo, considering the possibility of the ministry's falling, had asked Lucena to ascertain Deodoro's attitude toward a new ministry. The response of the marshal had been: "given a change of ministry, the government could consider the question ended and could depend upon the army entirely."[43]

On May 18, 1887, Silveira Martins presented the following motion to the Senate:

It is resolved that, in view of the imperial resolution of November 3, 1886, taken after the decree in council of the Supreme Military Council of October 18, 1886, the Senate invite the government to terminate the effects of disciplinary punishment made prior to the resolution against military personnel for use of the press without prior approval, except in cases specified in said decree of the Supreme Military council as contrary to the discipline of the army.[44]

One Brazilian historian, Max Fleiuss, asserts that the republic was as good as established on the date of the passage of the above resolution.

Franco de Sá, a former minister of war and one of the instigators of conflict, led the heated debate over the proposal. Senator Octaviano, a Liberal, supported the motion by pointing out that during the early years of the empire the Senate had frequently collaborated with the government in similar circumstances. Ouro Preto, pointing an accusing finger at the Liberal faction which was seeking to cause further embarrassment to the ministry, said, "The Liberal Party cannot

42. Rocha Pombo, X, 70.
43. *Ibid.*, X, 71; Monteiro, *Pesquisas e depoimentos* . . . , p. 160.
44. Fleiuss, *História administrativa* . . . , p. 421; *Jornal do Comércio* (Sept. 7, 1922), p. 401; Vianna, "A queda do império," p. 862.

wish that the road to the power be opened for it by the swords and bayonets of the army."[45] He was supported by Silveira Martins who urged that the Liberals join the Conservatives in solving the question. After explaining that the elements involved in the question went beyond party lines, he concluded with the prophetic statement, "If a crisis exists, it is not of party, it is of institutions." Sufficient Liberal support was obtained for passage of the proposal and the ministry did not fall, although, in the opinion of Cotegipe, it suffered "some scratches in its dignity."[46]

It is possible that the monarchy would have survived beyond 1889 had the Cotegipe ministry of "scratched dignity" fallen. To the eye of the casual observer the question might have appeared settled, but a keen observer of the trends would have recognized it for what it was, an armistice. Affonso Celso, a Liberal leader and a monarchist, was not optimistic about the situation. After the passage of the Senate resolution, when Andrade Figueira, a Conservative, remarked that "It is only now that the war begins," Affonso Celso replied that he agreed with the observation and added, "The military question is very much advanced; dead, no."[47]

Cotegipe, having suffered the wrath of the military leaders, immediately sought to neutralize the position which they had assumed in Brazilian politics. Action was taken against officers and students of the Military School who had been active in the recent insubordination. Many students were expelled. Officers who, because of opposition to the ministry in Rio Grande do Sul, had been ordered to report to the capital were either retained on duty in the capital or were sent to distant provinces. Lieutenant Colonel Madureira was ordered to proceed to Sergipe as an inspector of infantry. Resentment lingered in the minds of the military, although no further serious conflcts occurred during the remaining months of 1887.

Early in 1888 the ministry was confronted with another military crisis. The police chief of Rio de Janeiro had long been a creature of the ministry in power; consequently the hostility between the ministry and the military created animosity between the police of the city and the military personnel. During February, 1888, Lieutenant Captain Leite Lobo of the Brazilian navy was visiting in the home of a loose woman who lived near a Rio de Janeiro police station. When

45. Monteiro, *Pesquisas e depoímentos* . . . , p. 161.

46. Fialho, p. 86; Oliveira Lima, *Formação histórica da nacionalidade brasileira* (Rio de Janeiro, 1944), p. 225; José Carlos Rodrigues, "Religiões acatolicas," *Livro do Centenário, 1500-1900*, II, Pt. 2, 126.

47. Fialho, p. 89.

accosted by police, Leite Lobo, who was not wearing his naval uniform, informed the officers that he was a naval officer. However, the arresting officers paid no heed to his explanation and Lobo was severely beaten when he resisted arrest.[48] After being placed in the police jail, he was forced to submit to further indignities. When an adjutant general of the navy came to the police station to secure Lobo's release, the police lieutenant was so rude to him that it was suspected that the lieutenant was acting under orders from his superior officers. Before Lobo was released, an army officer and relative of the prisoner was also scornfully dealt with by the police lieutenant. The treatment accorded these officers angered the members of the Naval Club and caused them to send a protest to the ministry.

The ministry did not immediately answer the protest of the officers. After some delay it gave out the information that an investigation would be made. The investigation, when it came, discredited the testimony of the adjutant general of the navy and that of the army officer who had sought to secure Lobo's release. Both branches of the service were indignant, and the Military Club of Rio de Janeiro sent a message to the Naval Club informing it that "You may count upon our support."[49] The Naval Club then declared itself in permanent session until satisfaction was given for the offenses which Leite Lobo had suffered at the hands of the police. The government, confronted with this new conflict with the military, ordered that the police lieutenant who had commanded the station in which Lobo had been imprisoned be dismissed from the force. The Naval Club was not satisfied with the dismissal of the lieutenant alone, however; it demanded that the police chief of the city, Coelho Bastos, be dismissed as well. Meanwhile, near-riots were occurring in the streets of the city as a result of incidents between military and naval personnel and soldiers of the police. Because of these incidents it became necessary for the government to order the police to leave the streets and to ask regular army soldiers to patrol the city.[50]

The Cotegipe ministry sought to retain the chief of police in office, but the princess regent, yielding to the demands of the naval officers, dismissed him. This new blow to the prestige of the ministry and the rising clamor for abolition of slavery—to which the Cotegipe ministry was staunchly opposed—caused that ministry to fall.[51]

48. *Ibid.*, p. 90.
49. Galanti, V, 103.
50. *Ibid.*; Fialho, p. 92.
51. Galanti, V, 103; Vianna, "A queda do império," p. 863.

To the chagrin of the Liberals, however, the collapse of the Conservative ministry did not lead to the formation of a Liberal government. On March 10, 1888, João Alfredo, another Conservative leader, was asked to form a cabinet. The angry radical wing of the Liberal party then drew nearer to the Republicans and this combination courted the military and sought to create new incidents between the Conservative ministry and the generals. Despite this opposition, the new ministry was not seriously embarrassed until November, 1888, when the police of São Paulo clashed with the soldiers of the 17th Infantry Battalion. A soldier of this battalion was beaten by the police of the city, and his comrades, after revenging themselves, retreated to the battalion's quarters. The chief of police of the city, speaking to the officers of the battalion, reprimanded them for the conduct of the soldiers. The officers were incensed at the language used by the chief of police, and the battalion commander, Lieutenant Colonel Honorato Caldas, in an order of the day said that the police chief should have been thrown out of battalion headquarters.[52]

Soon after this incident the minister of war ordered the battalion to be transferred from the city. The police chief, during his tirade, had informed the officers that he would ask for just such action; therefore, the apparent compliance with the request of that official aroused deep anger among officers of the battalion. They appealed to Severiano da Fonseca, adjutant general of the army, and asked that the transfer order be revoked and that they be given justice in the matter. Criticizing the conduct of the chief of police, they demanded that he be discharged "for the good of the public service." The ministry supported the chief of police but wavered when Republicans and Liberals sought to use the incident to create another military question. The chief was dismissed from the force, but no reference was made to the circumstances surrounding the dismissal.[53]

When the opposition press hinted that the official had been dismissed at his own request and that the military's demands had been ignored, Severiano da Fonseca resigned his post as adjutant general of the army in protest.[54] The adjutant general's act complicated the situation and the government immediately changed its position. The ministry informed the adjutant general that although *O Paiz* had hinted that the official had been dismissed at his own request, such was not the case. *O Paiz*, a Republican journal, was only seeking to

52. Galanti, V, 104.
53. *Ibid.*; Rocha Pombo, X, p. 99.
54. Galanti, V, 104.

arouse the anger of the military class. "You may assure Severiano that the chief of police was dismissed by a decree of December 1, 1888, not at his request, but for the convenience or good of the public service."[55] The circumstances surrounding the dismissal were made known to the public, and it seemed that ministries of "scratched dignity" were becoming commonplace.

Following this embarrassment of his ministry, João Alfredo made a determined effort to end the military interference in the government. Marshal Deodoro and two battalions of the Rio de Janeiro garrison were transferred to Mato Grosso on the pretext that the province's military manpower had to be reinforced because of an impending conflict between Paraguay and Bolivia.[56] A rumor was current in Rio de Janeiro that the government, following the advice of Count d'Eu, planned to destroy the prestige of the Fonseca brothers. Deodoro was the unofficial leader of the military, and Severiano, as adjutant general of the army, was the official leader of the army. It was said that the government feared the influence of the two brothers and that once Deodoro arrived in Mato Grosso, Severiano would be forced to resign from the office of adjutant general. Obviously these rumors fitted into the Republican pattern of creating tension between the government and the military, but the logic of the government's move is evident.

Perhaps because of these rumors and of a desire to silence them, the government awarded Severiano the honorary title of Baron Alagoas. On the other hand, the ministry aroused the anger of Severiano through its continuous revision of the regulations for the Military School, regulations which the general himself had been asked to revise. On March 17, 1889, General Severiano conferred with the minister of war concerning certain regulations for the Military School. The two officials discussed the changes in the regulations and the minister assured General Severiano that the regulations which he had recommended would be adopted. The matter seemingly had been settled.[57] Two days later, on the morning of March 19, 1889, General Severiano read in the *Diário Oficial* that the minister had disregarded all of his recommendations. The angry general threw the paper to the floor and exclaimed, "This is an infamy!" It is possible that the ministry had sought to cause the general to resign his office, but the results of the betrayal assumed a more sinister aspect: soon after read-

55. Fialho, p. 95.
56. Lima, *O império brasileiro*, p. 160; Senna, p. 253.
57. Fialho, p. 97; Galanti, V, 105.

ing the article General Severiano died while taking his morning bath.[58]

In the distant province of Mato Grosso, Marshal Deodoro's resentment against the government's attitude toward his class increased when he learned of the death of his older brother and of the circumstances surrounding it. Remembering the wise council which the older brother had frequently given him, he exclaimed, ''The only person still able to restrain me is dead!''[59]

58. Fialho, p. 99; Galanti, V, 105.
59. Fonseca Filho, p. 33.

Chapter Six

The Ministry of June 7, 1889

The João Alfredo ministry, which had secured the emancipation of the slaves, was confronted with many difficult problems. When Parliament opened on May 3, 1889, one of the most acute situations facing the ministry was the alleviation of suffering of the inhabitants of Ceará caused by one of the worst droughts in the history of the province.[1] Other problems confronting the ministry were revision of the civil code, reform of local administration, revision of the land laws, promulgation of a new penal code, and revision of the regulations for the army and the navy. These and other reforms proposed by the Alfredo ministry were designed to safeguard the monarchial institutions of Brazil against the assault of Republican newspapers and orators.

The emancipation law of May 13, 1888, had strengthened the Republican party. It is true that the disgruntled former slaveowners did not take up the Republican banner, but the fact that they no longer supported the dynasty weakened the monarchist element. In the face of the growing Republican sentiment the ministry had need of the support of a united Conservative party. But the Conservatives had become divided into two hostile groups.[2] On May 2, 1889, João Alfredo, aware of the impossibility of achieving his aims, requested that his ministry be dismissed, but Dom Pedro refused to accept the ministry's resignation.[3] However, the chronic inertia of the Conservatives, who seemed "discontented with the present without having hope for the future," and the rapid increase in Republican sentiments forced the Emperor to call the Liberal party to power on June 7, 1889.[4]

Affonso Celso, Viscount Ouro Preto, one of Brazil's most astute statesmen, was selected to form what proved to be the last ministry

1. Alceu De Lellis, "O nordeste brasileiro," *Sociedade de Geografia do Rio de Janeiro, Geografia do Brasil*, I, 24.
2. Ouro Preto, "Advento da dictadura militar . . . ," p. 81.
3. *Jornal do Comércio* (Sept. 7, 1922), p. 395.
4. Ouro Preto, "Advento da dictadura militar . . . ," p. 81.

of the Brazilian Empire. This son of the mountainous province of Minas Gerais was gifted with that energy possessed by men who are accustomed to struggling against nature for survival. Ouro Preto, tall and heavily built, possessed a keen intellect and had the ability to express his ideas forcefully and clearly. Pince-nez glasses rested upon his strong, eagle-like nose, beneath which a long, already graying mustache waved challengingly at the members of the opposition. He had revealed his great administrative ability during the Paraguayan War when he served as minister of the navy. As a leader of the Liberal party during the years following the war he became one of the most skilful of Brazil's statesmen. "Excellent ally, terrible enemy, all feared him, great and small, rich and poor, fellow party members and opponents. He was not easily drawn into a struggle, but when he accepted it, it was to crush his opponent without pity."[5] When the Liberal party returned to power from 1878 to 1885, he had served as minister of the interior during the entire period. During 1886-1887, when the conflict with the military was rocking the foundations of the empire, he had been one of the first of his party to advise unity in the face of the bayonets of the army and to oppose the rise of the Liberals to power with the aid of the rebellious generals. It was to the strong intellect and skilful courage of this man that the weakened and failing empire looked for salvation.

The ministry of Ouro Preto contained three members who immediately drew the fire of the opposition. The minister of empire, Baron Lareto, was looked on as a minion of the Princess Isabel. General Viscount Maracaju, minister of war, was intimately connected with the family of Baron Lareto and was regarded as a staunch supporter of imperial policies. And Baron Ladario, minister of the navy, having no intimate connections with the court, was feared because of his influence with the senior naval officers.

The program which the new minister took to the House of Deputies was designed to make the establishment of a republic unnecessary. In Ouro Preto's opinion Republican agitation sought to institute a change in the form of government which would expose the country to grave misfortune, since Brazil was not prepared for government by the people.[6] Recognizing the menace of Republicanism he said:

It is necessary not to despise that torrent of false and imprudent ideas, but to accomplish the desired ends by weakening it, making it unnecessary, not permitting it to grow. The means of accomplishing

5. Fialho, p. 61.
6. Ouro Preto, ''Advento da dictadura militar . . . ,'' p. 162.

this are not oppression or violence; they consist simply in the practical demonstration that the present system of government has elasticity enough to admit the inclusion of the most advanced principles, satisfying all of the demands of the people, establishing liberty, and realizing the prosperity and greatness of the country without disturbing the internal peace of the country in which we have lived for so many years.[7]

The program of reforms which he deemed suitable to stabilize the monarchy and which had been approved by a caucus of the Liberal party included extension of suffrage to all literate citizens, enlargement of the electoral districts, full autonomy to the cities and provinces, augmentation of the right of assembly, freedom of religion, abolition of the life Senate, reform of the political nature of the Council of State, freedom of education, reduction of export duties, reform of agrarian legislation, development of rapid communication, and promotion and establishment of banks to aid the agricultural interests which had been weakened by abolition.[8]

The president of the ministry was not permitted to complete the presentation of his program without interruption from members of the opposition. The reference to the election of senators for a specific term in office was greeted with the cry: "That should be first. It can be done in the present session." Ouro Preto replied that he did not doubt that it could be passed in that session, but he stated that it would have to be passed after half of the other measures were considered. Pedro Luiz of the House of Deputies sarcastically added, "And after the beginning of the republic."[9] The minister interrupted the presentation of his program to answer the remark. "No, it makes the republic unnecessary. We can obtain the most ample liberty with the greatest ease and assurance under the representative constitutional monarchy."[10]

When the minister concluded his address Republican agitators shouted from the galleries: "Agents of the Palace! Courtiers! Personal government!"[11] Two members of the House of Deputies arose and announced their rejection of the monarchist ideal. They were Cesario Alvim, a Liberal, and João Manoel, a Conservative. The latter characterized the government as one of constant deception and referred to Dom Pedro as the *grande artista*. He concluded his change

7. *Ibid.*
8. *Ibid.*, pp. 163-164.
9. *Ibid.*, p. 164.
10. *Ibid.*
11. Fialho, p. 66.

of political faith with the revolutionary cry of "Down with the monarchy, long live the republic!"[12]

Ouro Preto energetically answered the challenge: "Long live the republic, No! Long live the Monarchy! The form of government which the great majority of the Nation favors and the only form of government which can make it happy and great!"[13] Replying to the charges that his was a ministry of courtiers, he pointed out that the merit which the members of the cabinet had earned in other fields, that is, away from the palace, had caused them to be invited to become a part of the present ministry.

The Republicans accepted the challenge offered by the program of the ministry. The journals of their party increased the tempo of their attacks upon the monarchy. After the presentation of the program of the ministry the *Diário de Notícias* accurately observed that "The events rush headlong toward the republic, more hurriedly than they advanced toward abolition. Federation would have been the preservative. Delaying it, the cabinet is destined to be probably the eliminator of the third reign, the last ministry of the monarchy."[14] This journal, edited by Aristides da Silveira Lobo, the man who was to become minister of the interior under the Republican regime, was joined in its attacks upon the ministry by *O Paiz*, edited by Quintino Bocayuva, future minister of foreign affairs of the republic. These two journals, edited and controlled by "practical men" who were willing to accept any solution which would lead to the establishment of the republic, took advantage of every opportunity to arouse the anger of the military class against the government.[15] They exaggerated and twisted news events so as to embarrass the government. Later, during the final months of the monarchy, stories detecting imaginary offenses against the military by government officials appeared in the journals.[16]

The program of liberal reforms designed by Ouro Preto to restore faith in the dynasty and to end the economic crisis of Brazil was not permitted to demonstrate its effectiveness. It is possible that these political and economic reforms would have delayed the establishment of the republic until after the death of the Emperor had the opposi-

12. *Ibid.*; Ouro Preto, "Advento da dictadura militar . . . ," p. 167.
13. Ouro Preto, "Advento da dictadura militar . . . ," p. 167.
14. Fialho, p. 67.
15. Monteiro, *Pesquisas e depoimentos* . . . , p. 301; Carlos Maximiliano, *Comentários a constituição brasileira* (Porto Alegre, 1929), p. 73.
16. Ruy Barbosa, *Finanças e política da república* (Rio de Janeiro, 1892), p. 278; Ouro Preto, "Advento da dictadura militar . . . ," p. 31.

tion parties permitted the program to be executed. Republican action and Conservative inertia forced Viscount Ouro Preto to pass over from a defensive effort to save the monarchy to the offensive. Astute statesman though he was, Ouro Preto was not the type of man to conduct such an endeavor. In the face of a military dissatisfied and needled by Republican agitators, his challenging and impetuous temperament was "an aggravating element."[17] The situation was one which demanded a man who could compromise with the military, one who would grant concessions to the opponents of the government, and one who closely observed the changes in popular feelings.

The House of Deputies failed to give support to the proposals made by the president of the ministry, and that legislative body was dissolved. New elections were announced for August 31, 1889, and in accordance with the machinations which had prevailed throughout the empire period, the ministry at that time easily won a majority in the newly elected House of Deputies. Those reforms which the cabinet could complete without the aid of the deputies were attempted. The new ministry devoted considerable effort to the improvement of the economic condition of the country. New banks were organized and encouragement was given to all commercial enterprises. Commercial treaties were made with various countries for the purpose of opening new markets for Brazilian products.[18] While making these efforts to cure the country's economic ills, the ministry did not turn its back upon the challenge of the Republicans and the truculence of the military class. Ouro Preto faced each incident in a forthright manner and dealt sternly with the opponents of his ministry. It is even suspected that some incidents were instigated by the ministry in order to teach a lesson to the Republicans and their military allies.

Soon after the dissolution of the House of Deputies, on June 15, 1889, when the Emperor was leaving a theater, Alexandre Valle, a young unemployed clerk of Portuguese origin who was in the lobby of the theater, shouted "Long live the republic!" Although this demonstration was made in the midst of the after-theater crowd, few people noticed it because such display of revolutionary sentiment had become common. Valle followed the Emperor to the street and soon after he entered his carriage the young man fired a shot into the air. He then entered a nearby café where he loudly declared that he had attempted to kill the Emperor and remarked that when he

17. Vianna, "A queda do império," p. 864.
18. René Courtin, *Le probleme de la civilization économique au Brésil* (Paris, 1941), p. 84; Ouro Preto, "Advento da dictadura militar . . . ," p. 83.

tried again his aim would be steadier. Valle made no effort to escape, and finally two journalists reported the incident to a policeman who arrested the would-be assassin.[19]

It was suspected that Valle was a tool of the police. Whether this is true or not, the police took advantage of the incident in order to intimidate the Republicans of the city. On June 16, 1889, in an editorial in one of the newspapers, the chief of police prohibited vocal demonstrations advocating the establishment of the republic. At the same time agents of the police, armed with clubs and knives and protected by cavalry patrols, were sent into the streets with instructions to shout "Down with the republic, long live the monarchy!" This attempt to intimidate the Republican opposition increased the tension within the city.

The Valle incident was followed by another which had many of the aspects of a comic opera. The students of the medical college were accustomed to meet in a square near the college during the periods between classes. There they purchased oranges from an old woman who kept a stand. One day the carriage of a minister of the empire passed and the students, rather enthusiastically, gave a *viva* for him. The minister, displeased, prohibited the sale of oranges in the square. The angry students organized a huge protest parade which passed through the principal streets of the city. Students participating in the parade, which was led by the old woman orange peddler, carried oranges on the points of sticks or upon their hats. As they marched through the streets they shouted "Viva a laranja!" ("Long live the orange!")[20]

An incident of a more serious nature occurred during July. Viscount Ouro Preto entered the offices of the minister of the navy and passed three young naval officers who were seated in an outer office. These officers, seeing the minister, stood but did not remove their caps. This was in accordance with military tradition, but the viscount censured them and charged them with having failed to render proper respect to a superior officer. The Republican press took advantage of this incident in order to widen the breach which was developing between the ministry and the military. Although these incidents were of no major importance, they were a fruitful source of propaganda for the opposition press.

Viscount Ouro Preto during the entire period of his ministry seemed strangely unaware of the extent of the military's dissatis-

19. Rocha Pombo, X, 101.
20. Galanti, V, 106; Fialho, pp. 108-109.

faction. After his exile he declared that it never occurred to him that the false rumors which were published in the Republican press could have an effect upon the officers of the army and navy who had always been so correct and circumspect in the discharge of their duties.[21] The minister seemed to consider that the military had won the concessions which they had demanded. Senna Madureira and Cunha Mattos had been vindicated, the right of the military to air their discontent in the press had been recognized, and the hated Cotegipe ministry had fallen. In addition to these factors, the long line of *casaca* occupants of the ministries of navy and war had been ended by the ministry of June 7, when Baron Ladario and Viscount Maracaju were assigned to the ministries of navy and war, respectively. Another concession had been granted to the military when at the suggestion of the minister of war, Marshal Deodoro and the battalions under his command were ordered to return to Rio de Janeiro from Mato Grosso.[22]

It is possible that Ouro Preto's failure to perceive the depth of the animosity of the military made him appear bold and arrogant in the eyes of the army when he advanced a series of moves intended to end the military's interference in the government. He increased the strength of the police of Rio de Janeiro and organized a national guard for that city. At that time Rio de Janeiro had 500,000 people and the increase in the number of police to 1,400 men was not excessive for a city of that size and population.[23] This explanation seemed reasonable when it appeared in Ouro Preto's manifesto, published in Lisbon after his exile from Brazil. However, Republican agitators in the capital city regarded the move as an indication of the sinister designs of the minister. Ouro Preto himself frankly stated the mission of the newly organized national guard. "The reorganization of the corps of police and of the national guard was intended to satisfy immediately a need recognized by all. Their purpose was to execute the law and at the same time not to leave the government at the mercy of the troops of the regular army."[24] The reorganization of the guard could not be regarded as a threat unless the army nourished hidden plans for revolt.

During the spring months of 1889, Republican opposition to the ministry was intensified when rumors circulated in Rio de Janeiro

21. Ouro Preto, ''Advento da dictadura militar . . . ,'' p. 32.
22. *Ibid.*
23. *Ibid.*, p. 77.
24. *Ibid.*, p. 79.

that Ouro Preto had accepted the task of preparing the country for the abdication of Pedro II and the accession of Isabel to the throne of Brazil. The reinforcement of the police and the organization of the national guard were regarded as features of the plan to insure the accession. It was reported that the date selected for the abdication of the Emperor was December 2, 1889. Further credence was given the rumors because December 2 was Dom Pedro's birthday. On that date the national guard and the civic guard were expected to equal the strength of the army and to be able to assure the accession of the princess by force if necessary. The ministry, having been victorious in the election of August 31, 1889, would be able to institute its program of reforms and thereby forestall the establishment of the republic.

This was the political situation existing in Brazil on September 14, 1889, when Marshal Deodoro, still grieving over the death of his brother and resentful because of his long period of exile in the forests of Mato Grosso, arrived in Rio de Janeiro. The marshal was accorded a gala welcome by his comrades-in-arms and by the students of the Military School. The Republican journal, *O Diário de Notícias*, described the welcome to its readers in the following manner:

As soon as the packet bearing the illustrious and brave soldier anchored in our port many officers went out in steam launches to board it and to receive the marshal. A great number of citizens and military of the highest rank remained awaiting him on the quays. Among those who went out to the ship to greet the marshal was Marshal Floriano Peixoto, Adjutant General of the army. All of the officers of the 23rd Infantry Battalion were present on the quay and the band of that battalion played martial songs.[25]

During the many months of exile in Mato Grosso the marshal had had ample time to consider the status of his class in the *político*-controlled empire. Embittered by the circumstances which surrounded the death of his brother, and influenced by officers of his staff who had been nurtured upon the philosophy of Comte and who suggested that the establishment of a republic would assure just respect for the military, Deodoro at one time had considered taking his troops to Rio Grande do Sul and establishing a base of operations against the empire in that province. When he arrived in Rio de Janeiro he was suffering from a respiratory ailment. The condition of his health and the resentment which he still bore against the government caused him to delay his report to the Emperor for several weeks. When he

25. Fialho, p. 115.

did make his report, Dom Pedro confided to him during the course of their conversation, "I expect to see you commanding a great parade soon."[26] The opposition press seized upon this statement as a reference to the rumored abdication date and the expected elevation of Isabel to the throne.

During the afternoon of the same day that Marshal Deodoro returned from Mato Grosso, the Ouro Preto ministry became involved in an incident which reinforced the contention of the military that they were the victims of persecution and which furnished Republican agitators another opportunity to increase the tension between the military and the politicians. The incident, regarded in Republican circles as spiteful aggression on the part of the viscount because of the festivity surrounding the army officers' welcome to Deodoro, resulted in the confinement to quarters of Lieutenant Caroline, commander of the guard at the National Treasury. Ouro Preto had gone to the treasury building and had noted the absence of the commander of the guard from the group of sentries who protected the building. Informed that the officer was in the quarters reserved for him, the minister sent for him. When Lieutenant Caroline reported to the minister, Ouro Preto accused him of having been asleep. The accusation was denied, but the minister ordered the officer to confine himself to quarters. The lieutenant left the room and sought his superior officer so that the latter could relieve him of his command of the guard. Ouro Preto, noting that the officer had not gone to battalion headquarters, ordered a captain who was present to arrest the lieutenant. The confinement was extended to eight days when the officer violated the regulation against resort to the press in disputes between military officials and presented his complaints to one of the Rio de Janeiro newspapers.[27]

This incident was exaggerated in Republican newspapers. The viscount was accused of having degraded the officers before the soldiers of the guard. A contemporary opponent of the monarchy regarded that incident as an attempt to provoke a conflict which would involve Marshal Deodoro and thereby provide the ministry with an excuse for ordering his retirement. The incident was reported to be another trick designed by the Count d'Eu, who, Republicans claimed, was its instigator.[28] Although the viscount acted within his authority,

26. *Ibid.*, p. 112.
27. Vianna, "A queda do império," p. 865; Ouro Preto, "Advento da dictadura militar . . . ," p. 73.
28. Fialho, p. 116.

the lieutenant's delay in confining himself was legitimate to the extent that another officer should have been assigned to the post prior to Caroline's departure. It may be noted that Ouro Preto, by his conduct in this incident, demonstrated that he was no *político*—he was a statesman.

Before the flames kindled by the Caroline incident had subsided, a new clash occurred in Ouro Preto, capital of Minas Gerais Province, between military officers and the police of that city. The police chief of Ouro Preto ordered some soldiers to return to their quarters, and when the soldiers failed to do so they were fired upon by members of the police. The ministry's solution for this clash was to send the 23rd Infantry Battalion to Ouro Preto to replace the troops who had clashed with the police. Perhaps there was little relationship between the transfer of these troops and the reception which the officers of the 23rd Infantry Battalion had given to Marshal Deodoro on the date of his arrival from Mato Grosso, but the Republican press was quick to charge that the battalion had been selected for the transfer because of that welcome.[29]

While these incidents were increasing the tension between the government and the military, the Republican courtship of the man who was regarded as the leader of the military class continued. Before going to Mato Grosso, Deodoro had told a friend that he did not seriously regard the republican ideal because "A Republic in Brazil and complete disgrace is the same thing."[30] He said that he did not think the people of Brazil were educated well enough to have a republican form of government. A definite shift in this viewpoint was indicated on September 19, 1889, when he was interviewed by a reporter from *O Paiz*. On this occasion the marshal said that there were three Republican leaders in whom he had confidence, all of them young men of the province of Rio Grande do Sul. These were Assis Brasil, Ramiro Barcellos, and Julio de Castilho.[31]

A month after Deodoro's return to Rio de Janeiro, Republican proponents within the army had convinced him that a republic would end the persecution of the army and restore the military class to its rightful place in the nation. On October 12, 1889, Captain Adolpho da Fontoura Menna Barreto, who had recently returned from duty in Rio Grande do Sul, visited Marshal Deodoro in his home. During this visit the captain told of the despotic conduct of Gaspar da

29. *Ibid.*, p. 80.
30. Senna, p. 254; Fialho, p. 121.
31. Senna, p. 254.

Silveira Martins, Deodoro's old enemy, toward the military and the Republicans of Rio Grande do Sul. The captain fanned the flames of the marshal's hatred for Silveira Martins and said that the efforts of the government to lower the marshal's prestige had failed. The majority of the army stood ready to die with him in defense of the homeland.

Encouraged by the marshal's reaction to his suggestion, the captain consulted with his friend, Lieutenant Sebastião Bandeira. On October 16, 1889, these two officers returned to the marshal's home and discussed the lot of the military class with him. Deodoro was confined to his bed and was experiencing great pain. While the two officers were there talking with him, it was necessary for them to help him change his position on the bed. After listening to the two men for several minutes the marshal asked if Lieutenant Bandeira had been with him on the expedition to Mato Grosso. Not waiting for a reply the marshal mercilessly criticized the ministry because soldiers who had accompanied him to Mato Grosso were being transferred to the 7th Cavalry Battalion.[32] Lieutenant Bandeira indignantly remarked that he did not doubt that the ministry planned to increase the strength of the court guard and of the police of Rio de Janeiro. He accused the ministry of having increased the strength of the national guard and of having supplied the national guard and civic guard with equipment which it was unable or unwilling to supply to the army. Bandeira further asserted that the regular army would be reduced to one-half of its present strength.[33]

The idea that his beloved class might be destroyed by the maneuvering of the *casacas* aroused the anger of the marshal. Forgetting his pain, he sat up in his bed and shouted, as if addressing Ouro Preto himself: "No! I shall not permit this! The government shall go to parliament to give an account of such mistaken acts of patriotism! I will draw up the artillery and carry the seven ministers to the public square and deliver myself to the judgement of the people!"[34] Menna Barreto explained that if this happened the general would be the dictator of the republic. The two Republicans had now ascertained that in any crisis wherein the general must choose between the monarchy and the survival of the army, he would be willing to create a new government in which the army's posi-

32. Rocha Pombo, X, 112.
33. *Ibid.*
34. *Ibid.*, X, 113.

tion would be satisfactory. They left the general's home with the expectation that such a choice would be presented to him.[35]

On October 17, 1889, Menna Barreto and Sebastião Bandeira organized a demonstration in honor of Marshal Deodoro. The purpose of the demonstration was to permit the people of the city to see that the marshal's prestige and influence over the army had not declined. Menna Barreto and Bandeira invited the officers of the 1st and 9th Cavalry regiments and those of the 2nd Artillery Regiment to make a joint visit to the home of the marshal. That afternoon the officers met in the Campo da Acclamação and went from that place to the marshal's residence. Since the condition of Deodoro's health did not permit them to see him, they left messages indicating their support of the marshal's views. They then went to the offices of one of the Rio de Janeiro newspapers and gave an account of the visit. One of the officers who had participated in this demonstration, Captain Manoel Joaquim Godolphim, was given the responsibility of obtaining information concerning the marshal's health and daily informing the officers of the three regiments about his condition.

Many of the officers who had participated in this demonstration took an active part in the spreading of Republican propaganda among the soldiers of the three regiments. The argument employed to sway the soldiers was that they would benefit from such a change in regime, since the national guard and other units could not then supplant them.[36] These officers contacted enlisted men of staff rank, such soldiers as Sergeant Adjutant José Pedro de Oliveira Galvão, First Sergeants Agricola Bethlem and Arnaldo Pinheiro, and Second Sergeant Raymundo Goncalves de Abreu, who were urged to disseminate Republican ideas among the other soldiers of the battalions.

The suspicion that the government sought to lower Marshal Deodoro's prestige in the eyes of his comrades-in-arms or to cause him to commit a breach of discipline was seemingly confirmed on October 20, 1889. On that day the ministry dismissed Colonel Mallet, Deodoro's friend and companion since their service in the Paraguayan War, from command of the Military School of Ceará. The colonel was relieved of his duties at the school "for the good of the service," a clause which was employed only in the most severe cases of incompetency and insubordination. Colonel Mallet's dismissal had come following his request to be relieved of the command of the school after the government had refused to confirm his nomination

35. *Ibid.*
36. Fialho, p. 118; Ouro Preto, ''Advento da dictadura militar . . . ,'' p. 74.

of a subordinate officer for promotion. Immediately after its refusal to honor the colonel's request, the government had promoted the officer to a position higher than that recommended by Mallet.[37] The government's high-handed action in this case angered the military, but failed to force the hand of the man who three years before had said in a letter to Cotegipe regarding the apparent persecution of his class: "If Caxias were still alive, things of this nature certainly would not occur."[38] The incident only served as a source of additional fuel for the flame which Republican proponents had kindled in the minds of the officers.

Two days later, October 22, 1889, the most outspoken military disciple of Republicanism, Benjamin Constant Botelho de Magalhaes, spoke at the Military School of Praia Vermelha before the officers of the visiting Chilean cruiser *Almirante Cochrane*, his own superior officer, and the minister of war, Candido de Oliveira. Constant said that he protested against "the complaints of indiscipline, insubordination and disorder which the government parties constantly throw into the face of the military."[39] He added that the military would always be "armed citizens" but never *Janiçaros*. Not content at having made these insubordinate remarks, Constant concluded his speech by insolently challenging the government through his claim that it was "the undeniable right of the armed forces to depose the legitimate powers constituted by the nation when the military understands that its honor requires that this be done, or judges it necessary and convenient for the good of the country."[40] Constant had been a professor of mathematics for many years in the military schools of Brazil. As a leader of the Brazilian followers of Comte, he had been able to indoctrinate many of the younger officers with positivist concepts. Many of these officers and students looked upon him as one of Brazil's greatest men. This protest which he made on October 22 led the students of the Military School and many of the younger officers to shower him with flowers on the following day. In addition to this tribute they expressed their feelings of class solidarity. A further demonstration of class unity was made when the students of the Superior School of War sent a committee to the home of Marshal Deodoro to congratulate him on the improvement of his health and to express the admiration and respect which the students of the school felt for the marshal. During the week following

37. *Ibid.*
38. Fleiuss, *História administrativa* . . . , p. 417.
39. Galanti, V, 109.
40. Fleiuss, *História administrativa* . . . , p. 425.

his speech at Praia Vermelha, Constant continued to receive congratulations from fellow officers for his defense of the military class.[41]

When Ouro Preto learned of the breach of discipline which Constant had committed, he conferred with the Emperor about appropriate punitive measures, but Dom Pedro, who knew of the professor's revolutionary beliefs, said to Ouro Preto: "Benjamin is an excellent creature, incapable of violence; he is a man of $A + B$, and in addition to that, he is my very good friend. Send him to me and I shall speak to him with frankness and you will see that he will return to the right road."[42] But this "excellent creature" did not return to the right road, and he and other military men of Republican faith and the "practical men" among the historical Republicans rapidly began to instil in the minds of the military class the idea that a change of ministry would not solve their problems. The old Emperor himself must fall, they said, to end the persecution of the class and to insure that Count d'Eu could not get control of the empire. Benjamin Constant was assigned the task of altering Marshal Deodoro's viewpoint about the establishment of the republic and to cause him to relent in his desire to "accompany the old man's [the Emperor's] casket."[43]

Ouro Preto, oblivious of the danger which was threatening his government, was rewarded for his efforts to improve the economic condition of the country by the members of the Commercial Association of Rio de Janeiro. This association voted to erect a marble statue of the minister in the new building in the *Praça do Comércio* and to inscribe the date of his assumption of the presidency of the ministry and the dates of his decrees relative to creation of banks and issuance of paper money.[44] This action was taken on November 8, 1889.

On the same date that the association honored Ouro Preto, another group of men met to formulate plans which would lead to the minister's fall and exile. Deodoro, with the approval of Benjamin Constant, called a meeting in the Military Club for the purpose of discussing the transfer of the 22nd Infantry Battalion from Rio de Janeiro to the distant province of Amazonas.[45] While this unit was

41. Fialho, p. 120.

42. *Ibid.*, p. 426; Vianna, "A queda do império," p. 866. For a discussion of the trend of Comteism in Brazil, see J. F. de Assis Brasil, *Do governo presidencial na república brasileira* (Lisbon, 1896), p. 80.

43. Monteiro, *Pesquisas e depoimentos . . .* , p. 206.

44. *Jornal do Comércio* (Sept. 7, 1922), p. 384.

45. Senna, p. 251; Maximiliano, p. 75.

completing preparations for departure, the rumor was spread that all of the other battalions of the regular army would also be transferred to distant provinces. Lieutenant Caroline, the officer who had commanded the treasury guard at the time of the incident with Ouro Preto, had been transferred to the battalion which was to depart. After heated discussion it was recommended that the officers use their influence to insure the peaceful departure of the 22nd Infantry Battalion, but at the suggestion of Lieutenant Colonel Jacques Ourique, it was agreed that Benjamin Constant be given authority to make a final request that the government cease its persecution of the army.

On November 9, 1889, at another meeting of the Military Club, Constant urged the officers, who were incensed at the transfer of the battalion and of Lieutenant Caroline with it, to be calm and await a more appropriate moment to take action against the government. Constant considered that Deodoro's presence was essential for the success of any military revolt, and he urged that the government be given eight days in which to accord justice to the military class and to cease persecuting it. "Have confidence, gentlemen, in our own efforts, and if in these eight days the government has not done justice and ceased to persecute us, then I shall abandon the imperial family and will come to do my duty in the public square at your side."[46]

While this meeting was in progress the imperial family, the ministers, many of the officers of the new national guard, and representatives of the increasingly important commercial class entertained the visiting Chilean naval men at a ball on the Ilha Fiscal. The following day, a quiet Sunday, the 22nd Infantry Battalion crossed the city and embarked for Amazonas.

Aware that the transfer of the battalion would have a tremendous effect upon the attitude of Deodoro toward the government, Constant went to the marshal's home soon after the departure of that unit. There he complained of the state of the nation and particularly of the state of the military class whose discontent and sufferings could not be corrected by peaceful means. The measures which Constant outlined to the marshal indicated that a change of institutions was necessary for the improvement of the condition of the military class. Deodoro was of the opinion that the "situation was purely military and that it would be enough for the army to overthrow the ministry."[47] But Constant, the disciple of Comte intent upon the

46. Fialho, p. 125.
47. Monteiro, *Pesquisas e depoimentos . . .* , p. 204.

establishment of a republic, made him see that any solution short of the overthrow of the monarchy would be a simple monarchist sedition and, like the revolution of April 7, 1832, would result in the return of the same disagreeable practices. Replying to Deodoro's question as to the status of the old Emperor, Constant said: "The revolution cannot stop respectfully before his throne, but if we are victorious the emperor must be treated with all of the consideration due to his state of health and to his age. His family will also be treated well; we do not make war upon persons."[48] Then Constant requested that Deodoro consider the magnitude of the move which he was about to make and added that the advent of a republic in Brazil was inevitable. Should the marshal accept the leadership of the movement, much needless bloodshed would in all probability be avoided. Deodoro by leading such a movement would be displaying more patriotism than if he avoided participation in the revolution. Constant then discreetly left the room to give the marshal time to think over the proposal.[49] After conversing with the marshal's wife for a few minutes, Constant returned to Deodoro's room and found him in a thoughtful and bitter mood. After a long silence the general said: "Benjamin, the old man [Pedro II] is not himself, because if he were, he would not permit this persecution of the army, therefore since there is no other remedy let the monarchy be overthrown! There is no more to be expected of it; then let the Republic come!"[50]

Having obtained the essential support of the marshal, Constant sought out his friends among the army officers and arranged for a meeting of the leaders of the movement at Deodoro's home on Monday, November 11. He had already made contacts with civilian Republicans, and in order to obtain the support of the people and to give the revolution the appearance of being more than a military uprising, he invited Quintino Bocayuva and Ruy Barbosa, editor of *O Paiz*, to be present at the meeting.[51] The prominent Paulista Republicans, Francisco Glycerio and Aristides Lobo, were also invited to participate in the discussion. In the presence of these civilians and of the officers, Benjamin announced the decision which he and the marshal had reached at their conference the preceding night. Ruy Barbosa, addressing his remarks to Marshal Deodoro, said, "General, the armed forces cannot intervene in the internal policy

48. Fialho, p. 128.
49. *Ibid.*, p. 129.
50. *Ibid.*
51. "Fragmento de um artigo do Sr. Ruy Barbosa," printed in *Jornal do Comércio* (Feb. 15, 1892); reprinted by Rocha Pombo, X, 36.

of the country, setting up and overthrowing ministries. That would be a seditious position, incompatible with military loyalty . . . , and the army's natural mission.''[52] This editor and orator believed that when the constituted powers were destroying public liberty and ignoring the constitutional guarantees, ''the military should intervene as liberator of the homeland in order to make a political change.''[53]

This reasoning by the editor of *O Paiz* was acceptable to those ''practical men'' of the Republican party who were present at the meeting and to Marshal Deodoro. The Republicans pledged the support of their party. When Ruy Barbosa proposed that he announce his Republican faith in the next issue of *O Paiz*, the proposal was opposed because it was feared that such a move would serve as a warning to the government. Ruy Barbosa's political creed was one dedicated to federalism. He had sought a genuine parliamentary government for Brazil. ''Both monarchy and republic are only the means. Liberty is the true end. . . . If the monarchy cannot accept the radical forms suggested, the liberals will go over to the republican party. This is the only procedure left to us.''[54]

Without doubt the civilian Republicans who were present at this meeting were surprised at the tremendous effect their propaganda had had upon the military, and even then they began to plan ways and means to secure control of the country in order to gain the fullest benefits from the revolution which the army was about to make for them.

Meanwhile, efforts had been made to indoctrinate certain of the enlisted men with the plans for revolt. Cadet Sergeant Raymundo de Abreu Filho, having been a companion of many of the younger officers in the Military School, was selected as a leader of the movement among the enlisted men. This soldier had held a meeting with several other enlisted men on the night of the departure of the 22nd Infantry Battalion.[55] Abreu explained to the soldiers the plans which the officers were formulating for the overthrow of the monarchy. He obtained formal pledges from them that they would support the movement, and the members of the group elected Abreu as their representative at future meetings of the officers. Since rumors of the planned uprising were being circulated in the city during the

52. Fialho, p. 131.
53. *Ibid.*
54. ''As Influências Políticas Anglo-Americanas em Ruy Barbosa,'' a lecture delivered in Rio de Janeiro, March 16, 1942; quoted by Turner, p. 99.
55. Senna, p. 66.

days before the revolt, Lieutenant Colonel Silva Telles, a monarchist officer, on several occasions questioned the non-commissioned officers of the suspected regiments. Silva Telles told the soldiers that he knew all about the planned revolution and he urged them to remain faithful to the Emperor, telling them that their reward would be promotion to commissioned rank to replace those officers who were involved in the plot against the government. The soldiers denied having any knowledge of the plot and protested that since they were enlisted men they knew nothing of the plans of the officers.[56]

After the Monday night meeting in the home of Marshal Deodoro the organization for revolution was intensified. Young officers of the Rio de Janeiro garrison and of the military schools gathered written pledges of their support and delivered them to Benjamin Constant. It was the position of the navy which caused Deodoro and Constant the most concern, and at the suggestion of the marshal, Constant sought to obtain an understanding with the naval officers.[57] Captain Frederico Lorena was asked to speak to Admiral Wandenkolk and arrange for a conference between Constant and the admiral.[58] Captain Lorena was successful in completing arrangements for the conference and the two men met on the afternoon of November 12 in the Café de Rio on Rua do Ouvidor. During the following days Admiral Wandenkolk was able to persuade other naval officers to join the revolutionary movement. Through the efforts of the admiral and of other naval officers, the ministry lost the support of so much of the navy that the strength of the loyal forces was insufficient to cope with the army when the crisis of November 15 occurred.

The adjutant general of the army, Marshal Floriano Peixoto, was a man of immense prestige in the army, and because he had not made his position known it was feared that he could offer great resistance to any armed attempt to overthrow the government. During the first meeting to which the civilian Republicans had been invited, Constant had expressed concern about the position which Marshal Floriano might take. Marshal Deodoro had assured him that there was no reason to worry:

There is no difficulty there. Floriano has always joined in the military questions. He declared to me long ago that he would not put himself in anything for the overthrow of the ministry; however, he told me, putting his hands on the lapels of his uniform, *that the*

56. *Ibid.*, p. 67.
57. Fialho, p. 133.
58. *Ibid.*

monarchy is the enemy of this. If it must be overthrown, I shall be ready.[59]

Deodoro then told those who were present that anyone who spoke in that manner would have to be with them. Arrangements were made for Floriano to be invited to see the marshal.

In the interview with Floriano, Deodoro explained that his purpose was to avenge the insults which the military had received from the *casacas*. Floriano, prudent, cautious, and aware of the position of trust which he held in the government, advised moderation. He informed Deodoro that he did not think that things had gone far enough to justify a military uprising. "It is still possible," he said, "to have an understanding with the ministry." When Deodoro informed him that "the movement was irrevocable and that he already was leading his comrades," Floriano assured the marshal that "If I suspected for one moment that the government is persecuting my class, I would immediately resign and take my place at your side. In any case you know that above all I am a soldier and your comrade."[60]

On November 14, 1889, the day following the interview between Deodoro and Floriano, Viscount Ouro Preto received a letter from Candido de Oliveira, minister of justice, in which Oliveira said that he had received a letter from the adjutant general and that the latter had reported that "he feared something." The viscount upon receipt of this letter called a meeting at which the ministers of war and of justice and the president of the province of Rio de Janeiro were present.[61] Ouro Preto showed the letter which Floriano had written to the minister of war, but that minister could give no additional information about the adjutant general's fears. The minister of war stated that he was certain that all went well and he added that should anything happen the government could suppress any disorder because he was confident of the support of the First Brigade in almost any emergency.[62]

To the viscount's query whether Floriano could have been referring to something about Marshal Deodoro, the minister of war doubted that such could be the case, since the marshal was ill. But Ouro Preto continued to consider the marshal as a source of trouble

59. Monteiro, *Pesquisas e depoimentos* . . . , p. 207.
60. Fialho, p. 134; Rocha Pombo, X, 156; Ouro Preto, "Advento da dictadura militar . . . ," p. 48; Silveira Lobo, p. 129.
61. Ouro Preto, "Advento da dictadura militar . . . ," p. 42.
62. *Ibid.*

and he ordered that the adjutant general be sent to call on Deodoro and to note his attitude. The results of the call were to be made known to Ouro Preto at his home that night. Before the meeting was concluded it was agreed that should Marshal Deodoro fail to give a satisfactory explanation of his conduct, action would be taken against him, even to the point of having him resign his commission in the army.[63]

While the viscount waited vainly for Marshal Floriano to make his report about the attitude of Marshal Deodoro, he had ample time to reflect upon the incidents of the past few weeks, all of which seemed to indicate that a revolution on the part of the army could be anticipated. First had come the revolutionary statements of Constant, then the commendations which those statements had earned that officer. Soon after this incident, the viscount had been informed of the meetings of the officers in the Military Club. One of the articles in Ruy Barbos's *O Paiz* had criticized the tyranny of the government and had said that such action would not continue for an indefinite period of time, "thanks to the unavoidable proximity of the fall of the monarchy."[64] These manifestations of possible disorder had alarmed the viscount, although later in his manifesto, which was published in Lisbon, he declared that he had never believed a military revolution possible. Ouro Preto had called the attention of his cabinet to these disturbing trends during the last meetings of that body on November 12, 1889. He had recommended that the ministers of war and justice conduct an investigation and take whatever action their investigation revealed to be necessary. The minister of war on this occasion had told the viscount that there was nothing to fear, that "in the morning I shall speak to the adjutant general. . . . Do not worry; we are watchful, I and Marshal Floriano, nothing will happen."[65]

During the weeks preceding the military revolt, Republican agitators had loosed a storm of propaganda against the government. One of the most effective points of this campaign was the report that the government intended to divide the army by distributing the regular troops throughout the provinces of the empire. The departure of the 22nd Infantry Battalion for Amazonas on November 10 had given credence to this rumor, but Ouro Preto later affirmed that this battalion had been ordered transferred to that province at the suggestion

63. *Ibid.*
64. *Ibid.*, p. 43.
65. *Ibid.*, p. 41.

of Marshal Floriano.[66] The transfer of the 9th Regiment to Minas Gerais had been accompanied by the rumor that the soldiers of that unit were to be imprisoned in military fortresses through the country. This rumor caused the wives and relatives of the soldiers of that regiment to go to Captain Menna Bareto and plead that he prevent any such plan.[67] This "skilful and patriotic strategem of war" was utilized to remove the last vestiges of support from the monarchy and to convince the military of the necessity of the establishment of the republic.[68]

The tremendous effect of this strategy is seen in the interview between Ouro Preto and Souza Ferreira, editor of the *Jornal do Comércio*. The interview occurred in Ouro Preto's home on the night of November 14 at ten o'clock. Souza Ferreira asked the viscount if the rumor were true that orders had been issued for the imprisonment of Marshal Deodoro and for the embarkation of the regular army garrisons of the capital. Ouro Preto, not fully cognizant of the crucial aspect of the situation, informed the editor that the rumors were false, that the government had no reason to issue such orders. When the editor informed Ouro Preto that it was fortunate that such orders had not been issued because they would not have been obeyed, Ouro Preto informed the editor that orders issued by the government would have to be obeyed.

I affirmed before, and I repeat, that I recall no orders having been issued for the imprisonment of Marshal Deodoro, nor for the departure of any corps of the garrison of the city; but, if the convenience of the public service require it, I would not hesitate in giving the necessary orders, whatever the consequences. Were I disobeyed, I would have recourse to the battalions which remain loyal, recourse to the navy, to the national guard and to the people; in any case I would do my duty. It is necessary to maintain power with dignity, otherwise I would resign my office.[69]

When the editor requested permission to print a denial of the rumors in the pages of the *Jornal do Comércio*, Ouro Preto said that he would give permission for that to be done. However, when Souza Ferreira asked that Ouro Preto have a denial of the rumors printed in the *Diário Oficial*, the viscount refused: "I will not do it, because that would oblige me to deny all the rumors which the opposition

66. Ottoni, p. 105; Ouro Preto, "Advento da dictadura militar . . . ," p. 106.
67. Senna, p. 66.
68. Ouro Preto, "Advento da dictadura militar . . . ," p. 107.
69. Vianna, "A queda do império," p. 869; Ouro Preto, "Advento da dictadura militar . . . ," p. 44.

invents.'' The editor again referred to the rumors concerning the arrest of Deodoro and said that he sought only to do his duty as a friend and as a journalist who was interested in the maintenance of public order.[70] The confidence which Ouro Preto displayed in this interview was not shaken until the following morning when the support for the monarchy was crumbling about him, when there were no effective loyal military units, and when the people, unconcerned, ''stood by beast-like,'' seemingly unaware of what was happening while the military removed the last remnants of monarchy from the Americas.[71]

70. Ouro Preto, ''Advento da dictadura militar . . . ,'' p. 45.
71. Affonso Celso, *Oito Anos de parlamento* (Rio de Janeiro, 1901), p. 247; Vianna, ''A queda do império,'' p. 879.

Chapter Seven

November 15, 1889

During these crucial days Deodoro's health had not improved, and as late as the afternoon of November 14, 1889, Benjamin Constant, after a conference with the marshal, told Aristides Lobo that he feared that Deodoro would not be ready and that should the marshal die the revolution would be defeated.[1] The condition of Deodoro's health was causing grave concern to the members of his family. His sister, Dona Amelia, invited him to the home of his brother, Dr. João Severiano, with the hope that the change of atmosphere would be beneficial to him. Marshal Deodoro accepted the invitation and, accompanied by his wife, he spent a restful day. The improvement in his condition led his relatives to insist that he also spend the night at his brother's home. Deodoro's wife and one of her nieces returned home in order to get some medicine and to inform the servants that they would not return that night.

While making final preparation to return to João Severiano's home, Dona Mariana Cecilia saw a carriage stop at the front of her home. The occupant, Benjamin Constant, was admitted by the niece. After greeting Dona Mariana Cecilia, Constant asked if the marshal's condition had improved. While he was speaking she noted with surprise that several other men had followed him into the room. Among the newcomers was Percilio da Fonseca, one of her nephews. When Constant had been informed of the improvement in the marshal's condition it was decided that Percilio da Fonseca would go to João Severiano's home and request that the marshal return to his home at once. The young man departed on this mission at 7:30 P.M.; two hours later Marshal Deodoro, accompanied by the nephew, arrived and conferred with those who were present.[2]

Constant and other leaders of the movement had sought the marshal because rumors of the plot had circulated among the soldiers, thereby making it necessary to begin the revolt at once rather than

1. Monteiro, *Pesquisas e depoímentos* . . . , p. 213.
2. Senna, p. 256.

on November 20, the date originally planned for the uprising. During the early evening hours of November 14, Lieutenant Augusto Cincianato de Araujo had informed Captain Menna Barreto, whom he found in a coffee shop on the Rua do Ouvidor, that the ministry had met and that well-informed sources stated that it had been decided to imprison Marshal Deodoro immediately. The captain was also informed of the proposed transfer of the 7th Infantry Battalion and of the 9th Cavalry Battalion to remote provinces.[3] As soon as Captain Barreto learned of these rumors he set out for the headquarters of the 9th Battalion. On arrival at the unit's headquarters he inflamed the junior officers with the report of the impending arrest of Marshal Deodoro. His ardent, and perhaps theatrical, demand —"I want a sword and a uniform in order to show how I can die for the general!"—was an invitation to rebellion.[4] Aided by Lieutenants Nolasco, Joaquim Ignacio, Manoel Joaquim, and other officers, he supervised the formation of the 1st and 9th battalions. The 2nd Artillery Regiment was also formed and their heavy weapons were lashed to the horses. Ammunition was distributed to the troops. Thus, before 9 P.M. on November 14, three units filled with enthusiasm and shouting *vivas* for the republic and for Marshal Deodoro were in an open state of rebellion.[5]

The enthusiasm displayed by the men of the enlisted ranks indicated the effectiveness of the work of the staff non-commissioned officers who had been indoctrinated with Republican ideas. On November 12 and 13 Sergeants Raymundo de Abreu and Arnaldo, with other non-commissioned officers, had distributed copies of *Correio do Povo* and *Dia*, Republican newspapers which contained long articles describing the conditions which the monarchy permitted to exist within the army and discussing the prospective dissolution of the army and the rise of the national guard.[6]

Unaware of the rebellious attitude of the troops, Constant went to his home after he had conferred with the marshal concerning the rumors of the old soldier's impending arrest. The excitement of the early evening hours had caused Deodoro to suffer a new attack which forced him to bed.[7] During the remainder of the night Deodoro experienced great pain, but when messengers sent by Constant arrived

3. *Ibid.*, p. 62.
4. *Ibid.*, p. 63.
5. Rocha Pombo, X, 187.
6. *Ibid.*, X, 131, 210.
7. Fialho, p. 143.

to inform him of the march of the troops upon the ministry, he forgot his pain and said "Let us prepare ourselves and depart."[8]

While the leaders of the military, Deodoro and Constant, seemingly expected that the disorder in the quarters of the regiments stationed at São Christovão would subside and that the revolution would proceed in accordance with the original plan, junior officers, noncommissioned officers, and others were intensifying their efforts to precipitate the revolution. The struggle which was commencing between the government and the rebellious troops was a silent one. The people of the city of Rio de Janeiro slept tranquilly during the night of November 14, and only the troops and the government were aware of the rumors of the arrest and imprisonment of military leaders and of the grave consequences such rumors might bring to the ministry.[9] About 11 P.M. that same day, Lieutenant Colonels Silva Telles and Costa Guimarães entered the barracks at São Christovão. These two officers were met by some of the junior officers who had caused the troops to form. After inspecting the men, Silva Telles demanded to know who had ordered the formation. Lieutenant Costa Guimarães sought to point out to the troops that the army had no justifiable complaint against the government, and he asserted that the Republicans were using the military as a tool in order to accomplish their ends. Guimarães advised the troops to lay down their arms, and one squadron attempted to follow his advice, but Cadet Raymundo de Abreu ordered the men to retain their formation and he was obeyed.[10]

A few hours after the attempt of the lieutenant colonels to have the troops break formation, Major Solon Ribeiro, a strong advocate of Republicanism and reportedly the instigator of the rumors of the imprisonment of Marshal Deodoro, arrived at the barracks and said that he had been with Deodoro, Benjamin Constant, Admiral Wandenkolk, and Captain Frederico Lorena. He informed the troops that Marshal Deodoro desired the 2nd Brigade to be prepared to move at an instant's notice.[11] After giving this order, Solon Ribeiro called Lieutenant Colonel Silva Telles to one side and conferred with him. After that conference, the officers who were present, at the suggestion of Menna Barreto, gathered in a separate corner of the building and took an oath that the regiments would not lay down their arms and that at dawn they would march to the city for the purpose of over-

8. *Ibid.*, p. 145.
9. *Jornal do Comércio* (Sept. 7, 1922), p. 395.
10. Senna, p. 69.
11. *Ibid.*, p. 64.

throwing the government. It was agreed that any officer who demonstrated by word or by deed that he was opposed to the movement would be shot immediately.[12] The same procedure was followed among the officers of the other units involved in the revolution, including the officers of the Superior School of War.

Some apprehension was aroused in the quarters when Major Serzedello Correa arrived there with the information that all the infantry battalions of the garrison were opposed to the movement. He suggested that the movement be postponed, but the leaders who were present opposed any delay. Near one o'clock on the morning of November 15, Lieutenant Pedro Paulino da Fonseca, brother of Marshal Deodoro, Captain Hermes Rodrigues da Fonseca, and another relative of the marshal arrived at the quarters and informed the officers that the marshal desired the movement against the ministry to begin at daybreak, since only at that time could the imperial marines, who were supporting the revolution, be disembarked from their ships.[13] After listening to these orders, the officers commanded their troops to rest. At 4:30 A.M. the troops were called to formation and ammunition was distributed to those who needed it. At 5:30 A.M. Lieutenant Colonel Benjamin Constant arrived at São Christovão. Constant was accompanied by Lieutenant Lauro Muller and a bugler. He alighted from his coach exclaiming: "I am among my friends. I arrived in time to see who knows how to die for the homeland."[14] Noticing the smart appearance of the 1st Cavalry Regiment, he remarked: "There is still dignity in the military class!" The arrival of Constant in the quarters aroused enthusiasm among the troops and increased their desire to move out on the mission which the revolution's leaders had assigned to them.

Constant directed the preparation for departure from the quarters. He sent one messenger to the Naval Club to inform the naval officers that he hoped all of them would join the move against the government and that they would make possible the landing of the marines so that the latter could participate in the rebellion. Another message was sent to Marshal Floriano Peixoto, adjutant general of the army. Constant informed Floriano that because of the extreme illness of Marshal Deodoro, the army and naval units participating in the rebellion asked that he assume the command of the movement.[15]

12. *Ibid.*
13. *Ibid.*, p. 65.
14. *Ibid.*, p. 71.
15. Ouro Preto, ''Advento da dictadura militar . . . ,'' p. 58.

The nature of the movement had not been clarified, and even at this time Major Lobo Botelho, learning that the objective was the overthrow of the monarchy, declared he would not participate in any attempt to dethrone Dom Pedro II. Botelho ordered the troops under his command to unfurl the imperial flag and to give a *viva* for the Emperor.[16] This attempt to arouse opposition to the movement among the troops failed because Captain Porto, Lieutenant Saturnino Cardoso, and other officers silenced the major and forced him to surrender the imperial banner to Brigadier José Ribeiro, who passed it on to one of the non-commissioned officers, Sergeant Bustamente. Major Lobo Botelho had not been alone in his assumption that the movement was against the cabinet; many of the soldiers and officers who departed from São Christovão on the morning of November 15 believed that they marched forth to overthrow a ministry. Soon after the Lobo Botelho incident, Constant mounted a horse and was joined by Silva Telles, the officer who earlier in the night had attempted to make the troops lay down their arms. The two officers led the men out of the quarters and toward the city.[17]

While Republican officers were spreading the rumors which enabled them to lead the regiments stationed at São Christovão in rebellion, the ministry was rapidly becoming aware of the seriousness of the disaffection of the military class. The action which had occurred in the quarters at São Christovão had not occurred without the government's receiving information about the preparation for revolution. At 11:45 P.M. on November 14 the chief of police of Rio de Janeiro informed Ouro Preto by telephone that he had been warned that the 1st Regiment was in arms. He also informed the adjutant general, and arrangements were made for the leaders of the government to meet in the army headquarters building.[18]

Ouro Preto, accompanied by his aide, Colonel Gentil José de Castro, immediately left for the offices of the minister of war. He stopped at the office of the chief of police, and while there he learned that the cause of the revolt was the rumor of the imprisonment of Marshal Deodoro and the report that the soldiers were about to be attacked by the civic guard.[19] Marshal Floriano Peixoto and the commandant of the police of the province appeared at the office of the chief of police soon after Ouro Preto's arrival. Floriano gave additional information about the revolt and told Ouro Preto that

16. Senna, p. 72.
17. *Ibid.*
18. Ouro Preto, ''Advento da dictadura militar . . . ,'' p. 45.
19. *Ibid.*, p. 46.

Captain Godolphim had come to his home and had informed him of the efforts of Lieutenant Colonel Silva Telles to have the troops lay down their arms and of the subsequent acceptance of command of a portion of the troops by Silva Telles. Asked why he had not arrested Captain Godolphim, Floriano said that he permitted the officer to return to quarters because if he had failed to arrive the troops at São Christovão, realizing that the government had been warned, would have immediately attacked. Floriano informed the viscount that he had sent orders to the 1st Brigade officers instructing them to disarm and to await further orders.[20]

Apparently Ouro Preto still failed to grasp the magnitude of the movement because he ordered the adjutant general to arrest the officers and soldiers who had taken up arms, and to imprison them in fortresses in various parts of Brazil until an investigation could be made and the offenders brought to trial. When Ouro Preto asked if there were sufficient loyal troops available to execute this order, he was told by Floriano that the government had only two thousand men on whom it could depend.[21] Floriano also told the minister that the part of the 1st Brigade commanded by Baron Rio Apa was friendly to the rebels and that he had full confidence in only the 10th Infantry Battalion.[22] He went on to say that any naval aid the government could secure would have a great effect upon the morale of the rebels, since the seditious troops expected to receive the support of the navy. Floriano suggested that the 24th Infantry, quartered in the fortress of Santa Cruz, be ordered to return to the city immediately.

After this conference with the adjutant general, the viscount departed for the Arsenal of the Navy. From that place he sent the following telegram to Dom Pedro, who was in the summer palace at Petrópolis:

Senhor, tonight the 1st and 9th Regiments and the 2nd Artillery Battalions, on the pretext that they were about to be attacked by the Negro guard and of Marshal Deodoro's having been imprisoned, armed themselves and sent a warning to the chief of staff that they are coming to avenge that marshal. The government is taking measures required to end the insubordination and to cause the laws to be respected. I am in the Arsenal of the Navy with my colleagues of Justice and of the Navy. (3:30 a.m.)[23]

20. *Ibid.*, p. 47.
21. Rocha Pombo, X, 166.
22. Ouro Preto, ''Advento da dictadura militar . . . ,'' p. 47.
23. *Ibid.*, p. 49.

It was discovered after the fall of the monarchy that the telegram never reached the Emperor, although it was received at Petrópolis and was sent to the palace. The viscount meanwhile ordered measures of security to be effected at the arsenals of Rio de Janeiro. Steps were taken for improving the defense of the Arsenal of the Navy. After the arrival of Baron Ladario, minister of the navy, Ouro Preto left other security measures for that arsenal to him.

Viscount Maracaju, minister of war, suggested that Ouro Preto accompany him to the army headquarters building where the emergency station of the minister of war was located. When Ouro Preto objected and pointed out that the Arsenal of the Navy could easily be defended and that it would be better for him to remain there where aid could more easily be secured, the minister of war informed him that ''The presence of your excellency is necessary in order to arouse the resistance.''[24]

Ouro Preto and the minister of war arrived at the army headquarters at 7 A.M. on November 15. By this hour the viscount knew the troops who were rebelling against the government had already left the barracks at São Christovão and were marching toward the city with the apparent intention of attacking the headquarters building. However, when he asked the minister of war if troops had been sent out to intercept the advancing rebels, the minister replied that this had not been done. Ouro Preto, although admittedly not a military man, realized that ''plain good sense indicated that the rebels should be attacked at different points, especially at street intersections, because in this manner they could easily be dispersed.''[25] He also noted the absence of other provisions for defense within the headquarters building. Houses adjacent to the building had not been occupied and barricades had not been constructed. The battalions within the courtyard of the building, instead of being prepared to repel an attack, remained with their arms at rest. There had been no distribution of ammunition, nor had the first aid station been set up. ''Those who observed that force might suppose that they saw only a parade, or troops accompanying a procession.''[26]

When these observations were called to the attention of the minister of war, he did not deny their accuracy. He did say, however, that no force had been sent to intercept the rebels because he did not have confidence in the loyalty of all of the troops within the build-

24. *Ibid.*, p. 50.
25. *Ibid.*, p. 51.
26. *Ibid.*, p. 52.

ing. As to the preparation of the headquarters and the adjacent area
for defense, that had been left to Marshal Floriano Peixoto, ''a
highly distinguished officer who would organize it in the best manner.''[27] The expressions on the faces of the officers and men in the
building impressed the viscount: they were not those of men who knew
their duty and who were determined to fulfil their obligations at all
cost. Instead, uncertainty and anguish were on their faces. Only
Marshal Floriano remained calm. Sword at his side, ready to mount
his horse at a moment's notice, he gave orders frequently in a low
voice to officers whom he encountered or for whom he sent.[28]

Although Marshal Deodoro had had a fainting spell at midnight,
he recovered sufficiently to confer with General Almeida Barreto, a
veteran of the Paraguayan War and for many years his own personal
enemy. General Barreto had decided that his dislike of the marshal
was less than his distaste for the rumored destruction of the army,
and he had come to Deodoro to pledge his support. The general
promised to place the troops of his command at the disposal of
Marshal Deodoro. At 2 A.M. Deodoro conferred with his brother,
Pedro Paulino, who informed him of the events which had occurred
at São Christovão. On receipt of this information the marshal sent
Pedro Paulino and his nephew, Captain Hermes da Fonseca, to the
quarters at São Christovão with the request that the troops remain
at their post until dawn when Deodoro would join them.[29]

When the men under the command of Constant set out from the
barracks on the morning of November 15, Lieutenant Lauro Muller
and Antonio Brazil, a student of the Superior School of War, were
sent to inform Deodoro of the movement of the troops. However,
when they reached the marshal's home they discovered that he had
already set out to overtake them. Lieutenant Muller and Antonio
Brazil, who were returning to their places with the troops, met the
marshal riding in a calash with the curtains drawn. The lieutenant
informed the marshal that Constant had received assurance from
Marshal Floriano that he could depend upon the support of the adjutant general.[30] When the troops en route to the headquarters building learned of the arrival of the respected and beloved defender of
the military class they saluted him with loud *vivas*. The knowledge
that the marshal, despite his critical physical condition, had come

27. *Ibid.*
28. *Ibid.*
29. *Ibid.*, p. 74,
30. *Ibid.*

to take his post as leader in the defense of the rights and honor of his class was a source of inspiration to the soldiers. Lieutenant Colonel Silva Telles sought to silence their shouts, but his commands were ignored by the troops.[31]

When the troops arrived at the Campo de Santa Anna, Marshal Deodoro descended from the carriage and mounted a horse which Cadet Eduardo Barbosa had been riding. After placing himself at the front of the troops Deodoro sent Captain Godolphim and a squad of six men to reconnoiter the area around the headquarters. He also ordered Silva Telles to proceed to that building and upon arrival there to inform Marshal Floriano that Deodoro wished to have a conference with him.[32] A short distance from the headquarters building the forces led by Marshal Deodoro were joined by the 10th Infantry Battalion.

The forces under the command of the marshal when he arrived at the Campo d'Acclamação at 7:30 A.M. consisted of the following troops: the 1st Cavalry Regiment reinforced by a detachment from the Superior School of War, commanded by Lieutenant Colonel Silva Telles; the 2nd Mounted Artillery Regiment, commanded by Major Lobo Botelho; the 3rd Cavalry Regiment (on foot because no horses were available) and the 9th Cavalry Battalion, commanded by Major Solon.[33] Just before their arrival at the headquarters building these troops were joined by the 10th Infantry Battalion, commanded by Deodoro's former enemy, General Barreto.

On the pretext of leaving the headquarters to halt the attempt of the students of the Military School to join the revolting troops, General Barreto had led the 10th Infantry Battalion from the building and had placed himself at the side of Marshal Deodoro. In the *Jornal do Comércio* of November 30, 1889, he explained his conduct in the following manner:

I resolved to offer my frank support to my meritorious comrades, Deodoro and Benjamin Constant, and to aid them on the glorious day of the revival of our rights in the solemn moment during which we demanded reparations for the offenses made against our honor. That is why I informed Major Serzedello at eleven p.m. on the fourteenth that I would take the most dangerous position. I marched at the front of 1,096 soldiers, ready to battle and in accordance with my formal promise, I received my old comrades at the place where I should have attacked them, not as enemies whose march I should

31. *Ibid.*
32. *Ibid.*, pp. 53, 75.
33. Fleiuss, *História administrativa* . . . , p. 428.

stop, but as friends whose hearts moved at the beat of generous sentiments, in the defense of a just cause. . . . To General Deodoro in the place of a fratricidal sword, I extended the hand of a friend and of an old comrade.[34]

Soon after his arrival at the headquarters, from a window Ouro Preto saw Captain Godolphim lead his scouting party into the area in front of the building. When the minister called the attention of the adjutant general to this group, he was informed by the minister of war that General Barreto was mounting his horse and that he would isolate and capture this advance unit of the rebel troops. Ouro Preto turned to that general and remarked: "I am certain that you will do your duty." The general in an ironical tone responded, "Assuredly, your excellency knows that I have always done my duty."[35] However, the scouting party commanded by Captain Godolphim was not surrounded, nor was it attacked. That small unit remained in front of the building and it was soon joined by the marshal and the forces under his command. The rebel troops immediately deployed for combat and trained their guns upon the headquarters.[36] Inside the building the viscount ordered that the enemy be attacked, and the minister of war repeated the order in a loud voice, but no attempt was made by any of the troops within the building to obey the command. "The government troops remained in the yard with their arms at rest; they did not move."[37] Near the entrance to the headquarters, government soldiers could be seen conversing from time to time with the advance units of the rebel forces.

Lieutenant Colonel Silva Telles left the rebel forces and entered the building. He brought a message from Marshal Deodoro wherein the leader of the rebel forces requested that he and Marshal Floriano have a conference. Ouro Preto, standing near Floriano and hearing the message exclaimed:

Conference! To be sure Marshal Deodoro has not received any military command from the government, he presents himself here at the front of an armed force, in a hostile attitude and demands a conference with the adjutant general of the army! Order him to retire and use force to make him comply with the order. That is the only decision of the government.[38]

34. Ouro Preto, "Advento da dictadura militar . . . ," p. 55.
35. *Ibid.*, p. 54.
36. Rocha Pombo, X, 181.
37. Heitor Moniz, "Estadista do império," *RIHGB*, CLI, 182; Ouro Preto, p. 56.
38. Rocha Pombo, X, 194.

While the viscount was shouting these heated words, shots were heard at the front of the building. For a moment it seemed that a battle was developing between the two armed groups. Such was not the case. The shots had been fired at Baron Ladario, minister of the navy, who had failed to obey an order to surrender when he approached the rebel troops. Ladario fired upon the troops and they answered his fire, wounding him. The baron's was the only blood ✓ which flowed in defense of the monarchy.   ╱

The inertia within the headquarters building aroused the disgust of Ouro Preto and he related afterward that several times he asked members of the military if they conducted themselves in this manner on the field of battle when the enemy was only a step away. After having repeatedly ordered that the rebel forces be attacked and having heard his orders repeated to the adjutant general, the viscount was asked by one of the young officers to consider carefully the responsibility which he was assuming. The young officer remarked that there could be a needless loss of human life.[39] When Ouro Preto reported these treasonable words to the minister of war, that officer asked, ''Don't you know who that is? He is the son of Viscount Pelotas.'' Then the president of the ministry confessed that he understood everything. He made one final effort to have the rebels attacked, but he was informed that the government forces could not expect to win because the rebel artillery was so placed that it could not be taken. Turning to the members of his cabinet who were present, Ouro Preto said, ''We have been miserably betrayed. You gentlemen are witness to the fact that my orders have not been executed.''[40]

Ouro Preto pointed out that the artillery could be taken with bayonets since its position was only a short distance from the building. Between the first and second shots from the guns, infantry could cross the space and destroy the gun crews. When the two military leaders objected and said that this could not be done, Ouro Preto remarked that in Paraguay Brazilian soldiers had taken positions which had been better defended than those occupied by Deodoro's forces. Marshal Floriano, answering the suggestion, said, ''Yes, but there we were in front of enemies and here we are all Brazilians.''[41] Hearing his remark, the viscount knew that he could

39. *Visconde de Ouro Preto* (Excerptos biográficos), Artigos publicados no *Jornal do Brasil*, en 1927-1928, *RIHGB*, CLVII, 182; Ouro Preto, ''Advento do dictadura militar . . . ,'' p. 57.
40. Monteiro, *Pesquisas e depoimentos* . . . , p. 249.
41. Rocha Pombo, X, 169.

expect no resistance from the forces within the building, and he decided to discuss the situation with the ministers.

After holding a conference with the ministers in the office of the minister of war, Ouro Preto agreed that resistance was useless. The following telegram was sent to the Emperor:

Senhor, the ministry, situated in the headquarters of the army, with the exception of the minister of the navy, who has been wounded and lies in a nearby house, having vainly ordered more than one time that the troops under its command dislodge the forces commanded by Marshal Deodoro, before declarations made by Generals Viscount Maracaju, Floriano Peixoto and Baron Rio Apa, that we cannot depend upon the troops within the building, nor is there the possibility of effective resistance, places in the august hands of your majesty its request for dismissal. The troops have just finished fraternizing with Marshal Deodoro, admitting him to the interior of the building.[42]

A few minutes after nine o'clock the defenders of the building had thrown open the doors at the command of Captain Pedro Paulino of the 1st Infantry Battalion and welcomed Marshal Deodoro who entered, still mounted.[43] The old soldier, accompanied by the members of his staff, received ovations as he passed the lines of soldiers within the building. Soon after the marshal's entry, the artillery lined up in front of the building fired a twenty-one-gun salute to signal the almost bloodless victory of the rebel forces.[44]

Although the decision of the ministry had not been made known to them, the defenders of the building had thrown open the doors and admitted the marshal. Followed by Benjamin Constant and other officers of the rebel force, Deodoro, now dismounted, entered the office of the minister of war. Observing the minister, his cousin Viscount Maracaju, the marshal said to him, "Good day, Cousin Rufino."[45] Then directing himself to Ouro Preto, Marshal Deodoro informed him that he had placed himself at the head of the army in order to avenge the great offenses and injustices which the government had committed against him and against the military class. He affirmed that only the military knew how to sacrifice themselves for the good of their country. Until that time, Deodoro told the minister, the politicians who cared only for personal gain had directed the country. Now, despite his illness, he had not been able to refuse the desires of the members of his class that he direct them in the effort to end this persecution of the military men.

42. Ouro Preto, ''Advento da dictadura militar . . . ,'' p. 58.
43. Rocha Pombo, X, 194.
44. *Ibid.*, X, 181.
45. Ouro Preto, ''Advento da dictadura militar . . . ,'' p. 59.

Deodoro made references to his services during the war with Paraguay, telling how he had fought for three days and nights in a swamp. He then informed the viscount that the ministry was deposed and that another would be organized in accordance with the recommendations which he would make to Dom Pedro II.[46] He told the officials of the government that they could all go home with the exception of Ouro Preto, "the most stubborn of men, but not as stubborn as I," and the minister of justice, Candido de Oliveira. Then, referring to the Emperor, Deodoro said, "he has my respect, I am his friend, I owe him favors. His rights will be respected and guaranteed."[47]

Ouro Preto, that "most stubborn of men," aware that his attempt to preserve the monarchy was confronting its most grave crisis, did not cringe before the eagle-like gaze of the old marshal. Replying to Deodoro's recital of the hardships which he had endured on the field of battle, the minister said:

It is not only on the field of battle that one serves one's country and makes sacrifices for it. Being here listening to the general at this moment is not a less value than passing some days and night in a swamp. I am aware of what has been decided in reference to myself, the general is the victor, he can do as he desires. I submit myself to force.[48]

Many of the followers of the marshal who had heard the statement of the intended exile of the viscount appealed to Deodoro. At the request of Marshal Floriano, Senator Candido de Oliveira, Miranda Reis, and Dr. Pizarro, a professor at the Medical College, the president of the council was permitted to leave the headquarters building.

The marshal's statements to Viscount Ouro Preto indicated that he had reverted to the opinion that the matter was "simply one for the military to overthrow the ministry." On three other occasions he had permitted himself to be persuaded that a change of institutions was necessary to end the persecution of the military class. Now, however, victorious in the overthrow of the ministry, he was reluctant to force the fall of the man who was his friend and to whom he owed favors. In addition to his own opposition to the deposing of the Emperor, there were others among the military who had come to the headquarters building with the expectation that only the ministry would be overthrown; they felt they owed something to the Emper-

46. *Ibid.*
47. Fleiuss, *História administrativa* . . . , p. 431.
48. *Ibid.*, p. 432; Ouro Preto, "Advento da dictadura militar . . . ," p. 140.

or.[49] There also had been little indication that the populace, who seemed to want the republic after the death of Dom Pedro II, would be willing to accept it now that it had been prematurely launched with the aid of the sword.

After informing the ministers of their dismissal, Marshal Deodoro gave orders that the troops under his command form a march to the Arsenal of the Navy. The objective of this display of force was to determine the position which the naval forces had assumed and to observe the reactions of the civilian population of the city.[50] That the marshal was concerned with civilian reaction to the fall of the ministry is seen in his order to an officer of the 2nd Brigade who had given a *viva* for the republic: "Leave such manifestations to the people!"[51]

The route of march selected was through the most heavily frequented streets of the city. The 10th Infantry Battalion and the detachment from the Military School had rejoined Deodoro's force before it left the headquarters building. Only one unit, an artillery detachment, remained faithful to the Emperor and refused to participate in the parade through the city. After Deodoro had placed himself at the head of the troops, Major Solon, an ardent Republican advocate, rode up to him and enthusiastically exclaimed that he would not silence the young officer.[52]

During the march Deodoro, seated upon his horse, was able to see that the people accepted the work of the revolution. "They did not cease for a single instant to make expressions of their pleasure, and loud evidence of their joy because of the fall of the ministry."[53] They shouted "Long live General Deodoro! Long live the army and the navy! Long live the republic and liberty!" Spectators along the streets applauded, and from the balconies and windows women saluted the "founder of the true independence of his country. Not a single voice was heard which favored the monarchy."[54] It seemed that the people who witnessed the premature fall of the dynasty accepted it as inevitable.

Nevertheless, some of those who observed the advance of the

49. Senna, p. 253.
50. Galanti, V, 120; Fialho, p. 152; Ruy Barbosa, "Restituicões históricas," reprinted from *Comércio de São Paulo* (Dec. 19, 1903), in *RIHGB*, LXXII, pt. 2, 143.
51. Rocha Pombo, X, 215.
52. Letter to D. Tulia Solon from Quintino Bocayuva, July 21, 1902; reprinted by Rocha Pombo, X, 200.
53. Fialho, p. 153.
54. Calogeras, p. 270; Fialho, p. 153.

troops toward the Arsenal of the Navy did not express such optimistic views of the people's acceptance of the fall of the ministry. Aristides Lobo said that he would like to have looked upon November 15 as the first day of the first year of the republic, but he could not do so. In a statement published in the *Diário Popular*, November 18, 1889, he wisely pointed out that what had been done could be beneficial to the country, provided that the men who controlled the government which was taking shape before the eyes of the people were purely military, because "there was almost no collaboration of the civilian element."[55] Lobo wrote that the people "stood by stupidly, beast-like, astonished, surprised, without knowing what was happening. Many of them sincerely believed that they were witnessing a parade."

When the troops drew near the Arsenal of the Navy, Baron Santa Martha ordered the gates to be closed and preparations to be made for resistance. However, Captain Ferreira de Oliveira, who favored the fall of the monarchy, heard the order and asked that he be permitted to leave the arsenal and speak to Marshal Deodoro. This permission was granted, and Oliveira approached the marshal and asked what he intended to do with the forces under his command. Deodoro replied that he came to deliver the naval forces under his command to the commander of the arsenal and to thank the naval officers for the services they had rendered to him.

When the commander of the arsenal received this message the gates of the arsenal were opened and the naval officers, accompanied by Admirals Wandenkolk and Foster, went out to meet the marshal. In front of the applauding soldiers and sailors the two leaders of the armed forces joined hands.[56]

The failure of the leaders of the military to make a pronouncement concerning the establishment of the republic caused grave unrest among Republican advocates. At 3 P.M., after the parade through the streets of the city, José do Patrocinio, a former slave and a fervent Republican, speaking before a crowd of civilians and members of the armed forces in the Municipal House of the city, demanded that the republic be declared.[57]

Marshal Deodoro had returned to his home at the Campo da Acclamação immediately after the display of force before the citizens of

55. Assis Brasil, p. 12; Ouro Preto, "Advento da dictadura militar . . . ," p. 140.
56. Galanti, V, 122.
57. *Ibid.*

Rio de Janeiro. The excitement of the strenuous events of the day and the failure to obtain sufficient rest the previous night had an extremely adverse effect upon his health. When he arrived at his home it was necessary for two of the officers accompanying him to assist him when he dismounted his horse. He also had to be helped into the house. His condition alarmed his wife, and after he had been placed upon his bed she ordered that the door be closed and that no one be permitted to see him.[58]

During the late afternoon hours of November 15, the fear that the "military leaders had considered the gravity of the situation and hesitated to cause the overthrow of regime" led Republican leaders to take immediate action, so that the victory which had been won for them would not slip from their hands. After holding a mass meeting on Rua Ouvidor, Glycerio led citizens of Republican faith to the home of the marshal with the intention of having him make a statement concerning the intention of the military.[59] The marshal's condition did not permit him to appear before the people, but Benjamin Constant came to a window and informed them that "the new government would in time consult the Nation in order to decide what would be its destiny."[60]

Meanwhile, rumors were spread that the Emperor had called upon Gaspar da Silveira Martins, senator from Rio Grande do Sul and also an old enemy of Marshal Deodoro, to organize a new government. Republican leaders, after listening to Constant, met with him at the Institute for the Blind, of which he was director and which also was located in the Campo da Acclamação. The discussion was lengthy, and Constant, saying that he was very tired and was going home to take a bath, rose from the group and started toward the door. However, the more ardent Republicans who were present insisted that he remain because it was necessary that a proclamation be written at once and that the ministry for the provisional government be organized. Constant stayed and the proclamation and list of officials of the new government were completed.[61]

Later, Marshal Deodoro declared that he had signed the two documents only when he was certain that the Emperor had called Silveira Martins to organize the new ministry. The bearers had been permitted to enter his house only after much persuasion of the

58. Fleiuss, *História administrativa* . . . , p. 435.
59. Vianna, "A queda do império," p. 872; Lyra, p. 285.
60. Vianna, "A queda do império," p. 872; Rocha Pombo, X, 183.
61. Fleiuss, História administrativa . . . , p. 436.

marshal's wife, for Deodoro was still suffering great pain. Quintino, Glycerio, Constant, and others pointed out to him the danger which all of them faced should he fail to proclaim the republic and should Silveira Martins become the president of the ministry. Benjamin Constant pointed out to Deodoro that "The general had the right to dispose of his head, as he understands very well, but it seems to me, that he had not the right to dispose of the heads of his companions who have taken an active part in the revolt against the government."[62] Deodoro later admitted that these words deeply impressed him. "I recalled that Silveira Martins who was to organize the new ministry was my hated enemy and that it could be expected that not only I but my companions would suffer the consequences of the restless spirit of Gaspar."[63]

Thus, the marshal, who had risen from his bed at dawn with the intention of overthrowing a ministry, became, through the skilful maneuvering of the Republicans, the instrument which overthrew the empire.[64] Despite the many times that the Republicans within the army had obtained Deodoro's commitment to the Republican cause, the man who had been expected to fill the spot vacated by Caxias, the Conservative general, remained a Conservative to the end. It cannot be denied that he had given serious thought to the establishment of the republic, but after its establishment he often declared, "I did not wish to proclaim the Republic; that was the work of Aristides, of Benjamin, and of Quintino."[65]

62. Vianna, "A queda do império," p. 873.
63. Fleiuss, *História administrativa* . . . , p. 434.
64. Rocha Pombo, X, 209; Oliveira Lima, "Sept ans de république au Brasil," *La Nouvelle Revue*, CI, 514.
65. Fleiuss, *História administrativa* . . . , p. 437; "A revolução de 15 de Novembro Contestação a Suetonio," *Jornal do Comércio* (May 18-20, 1904); reprinted by Rocha Pombo, X, 209.

Chapter Eight

Marshal Deodoro, Provisional President and Military Dictator

Immediately after receiving Ouro Preto's request that the ministry be dismissed, Dom Pedro arranged for a special train to transport him and his party from Petrópolis to Rio de Janeiro. At 1 P.M. he arrived at São Francisco Xavier station where three imperial carriages awaited him. There was no military escort. He and the people who had accompanied him on the journey from Petrópolis went directly to the imperial palace. At the palace Dom Pedro found the most steadfast friends of the imperial family, mainly former ministers and senators who had come to offer their services. He declared to them that the situation was not serious, "It is nothing; tomorrow all will be finished; Brazilians are like that."[1]

Ouro Preto had remained in the headquarters building until 2 P.M. because it was feared that should he leave the building he would be attacked by some of his enemies.[2] Accompanied by his son Affonso Celso, he went to the home of his brother-in-law, Baron Javary. The Emperor's military aide, Lieutenant General Baron Miranda Reis, found him there and informed him that Dom Pedro wished him to come to the imperial palace. Dom Pedro received the viscount with his customary courtesy and calmness. The minister renewed the request that he be dismissed, but the Emperor sought to persuade him to retain his position. Ouro Preto, aware of the gravity of the situation answered, "The only service which I can fulfill for your majesty at this moment is to give advice concerning the organization of the new ministry."[3] Ouro Preto then suggested that Silveira Martins be called to organize the new ministry. Despite the fact that Silveira Martins at that moment was not in the city and could arrive only

1. Fialho, p. 136.
2. Ouro Preto, ''Advento da dictadura militar . . . ,'' p. 61.
3. *Ibid.*

after a journey of two or three days, Dom Pedro approved the viscount's nomination.[4]

Ouro Preto in making this nomination and Dom Pedro in accepting it were not aware, evidently, of the effect that Silveira Martins' leadership of the government could have upon Marshal Deodoro.[5] The viscount knew that Silveira Martins was a very popular politician who had distinguished himself as president of the province of Rio Grande do Sul. He was a man of great talent and prestige who had many influential contacts with high-ranking army officers. He was regarded as an intimate friend of Viscount Pelotas.[6] After conferring with the Emperor, Ouro Preto returned to the home of his brother-in-law. At 6 P.M. the house was surrounded and the viscount arrested by Lieutenant Veiga of the army headquarters staff. He was taken to the headquarters of the 2nd Brigade at São Christovão, where he was imprisoned until the order was received for his deportation.[7]

Dom Pedro did not immediately seek to make contact with the leaders of the revolution, and, still not realizing the seriousness of the situation, he continued to transact the affairs of the empire. "I am not afraid. I am not a sailor on his first voyage."[8] However, his daughter Isabel, becoming more alarmed at the state of affairs, urged him to organize a new ministry at once. She also sought to discover the truth about the events which were occurring in the city. When Ouro Preto had gone to the palace to confer with the Emperor, he had had no idea that Deodoro sought more than a mere change in the ministry. "I did not know that the republic was proclaimed in the Municipal House during the time I consulted the Emperor. The truth is that I knew nothing of it and all the people around me knew nothing of it."[9] He had spoken to Dom Pedro only of the demand made by Deodoro for a change in the ministry. His advice that Silveira Martins be called to head the cabinet was given without the knowledge that Martins was a personal enemy of Marshal Deodoro.

At 9 P.M. Isabel succeeded in persuading the Emperor to call a

4. *Contribuições*, p. 887; Ouro Preto, "Advento da dictadura militar . . . ," p. 62.
5. Albuquerque, p. 62.
6. *Contribuições*, p. 887.
7. *Ibid.*, p. 888; Tacito, "Ainda a ultima sessão do conselho d'estado," *Revista do Instituto Histórico e Geográfico de São Paulo*, VIII, 218.
8. Ouro Preto, "Advento da dictadura militar . . . ," pp. 61-62.
9. *Ibid.*, p. 62.

meeting of the Council of State to consider the situation. The Emperor had seemed dazed all during the day, and Isabel thought that such a meeting would make him realize the seriousness of the crisis which was confronting the dynasty. José Saraiva, at the request of the Emperor, appeared and conferred with him at 9 P.M. He remained in the palace until 11 P.M. and then went to his home. After his departure, Isabel, with the consent of her father, arranged for a meeting of the Council of State. The meeting, the last one of that body, began a few minutes after 11 P.M.[10]

Dom Pedro himself presided.[11] It was pointed out that Silveira Martins was hated by the leaders of the revolution and that it would be inopportune to select him for the presidency of the new ministry. At this meeting Dom Pedro first learned of the proclamation of the republic and of the selection of officers for the provisional government.[12] It was suggested that since Saraiva had not been involved in any of the military questions he should be requested to organize the new ministry. Stating that he had followed his custom of requesting the man named by the retiring minister, Dom Pedro accepted the advice of the council and a messenger was sent to the Saraiva home.

Saraiva, after securing the Emperor's permission to solve the difficulty in his own manner, immediately sent a messenger to Marshal Deodoro. Dona Isabel informed Saraiva that Dom Pedro had sent several messengers to the marshal, but that none of them had been able to see him. Andrade Figueira, a friend of the marshal's family, undertook the task of having Saraiva's message delivered by way of his cousin, Major Tromposky. Dona Mariana Cecilia conducted the major to Deodoro's bedroom and the marshal was aroused from sleep. It was 3 A.M. After reading Saraiva's request that they have an understanding before a new ministry was organized, Deodoro turned to Tromposky and said, ''Tell Saraiva that he is late.''[13]

The change in selection of the president of the ministry had been made too late to save the empire. It is possible that the empire could have been saved had Dom Pedro gone directly to the army headquarters building when he arrived in Rio de Janeiro. Deodoro himself later admitted that had the Emperor appeared at the Campo de Santa Anna he did not know what he would have done. ''A sad

10. Tacito, p. 219.
11. *Ibid.*
12. *Ibid.*
13. Rocha Pombo, X, 170; Fleiuss, *História administrativa . . .* , p. 439.

figure I would have been had the old man [the Emperor], without even a guard, confronted me in the Campo de Santa Anna."[14]

On November 16, after the provisional government had obtained the pledges of support from the majority of the provinces of Brazil, the leaders of the government turned their attention to the imperial family. Since the afternoon of November 15, the imperial family had been confined to the palace under the observation of a detachment of troops commanded by Major Frederico Solon de Sampaio Ribeiro. On the afternoon of November 16, Major Solon delivered a letter to the Emperor signed by Marshal Deodoro. Deodoro informed Dom Pedro that his remaining in Brazil would be "absurd, impossible, and would provoke public disorder," and that the maintenance of public order required that, following the example set by his father on April 7, 1831, he must leave Brazil within twenty-four hours.[15]

The Emperor's reply to the order which banished him and his family from Brazil was a declaration of his devotion to Brazil:

In view of the written statement which was delivered to me today at three o'clock in the afternoon, I resolve, yielding to the force of circumstances, to leave with all of my family for Europe tomorrow. Leaving this beloved country, to which I have given constant evidence of unusual love and dedication, during almost half a century, in which I discharged the office of chief of state, absenting myself, then with all the members of my family, I retain the most happy remembrances of Brazil and ardently wish her greatness and prosperity.[16]

The princess also sent a letter expressing her sentiments to the president of the provisional government. Later that day when information was brought to the palace that the new government was making provisions for granting 5,000 *contos de reis* to the Emperor, Isabel said that the question of money did not matter to them: "what hurts me is to leave the country where I was born and which I love."[17] The imperial family was informed that it must leave at dawn on November 17, but Isabel pointed out that she could not leave without her children who were in the palace at Petrópolis. Colonel Mallet, who had delivered the messages, assured the princess that arrangements would be made for her children to be brought to Rio de Janeiro prior to her departure.[18]

14. Fleiuss, *História administrativa* . . . , p. 439.
15. Braz do Amaral, "O imperador e o proclamação da república," *RIHGB*, CLII, 477.
16. *Ibid.*, CLII, 476; *Contribuições*, pp. 888-889.
17. Rocha Pombo, X, 231.
18. *Ibid.*, X, 232.

At dawn on November 17 the imperial family was escorted from the palace to the place of embarkation, despite Dom Pedro's protest that he was not a fugitive slave and that he would not leave at that hour in the morning.[19] It was 3 A.M. when the party left the palace, and the crowds of people who had been in the square in front of the palace had gone home. The family was taken on board a steam launch which carried them to the *Parnahyba*, which was anchored near the Arsenal of War. The captain of the *Parnahyba* was ordered to remain in that place until the children of the princess were taken on board. On November 18 the *Parnahyba* anchored near the *Alagoas*, a ship which belonged to the Brazilian Steam Navigation Company, and the imperial family was transferred. The *Alagoas* arrived in Lisbon on December 7.[20] Dom Pedro, who had refused the settlement which the provisional government had offered to him and his family, was cordially received by Dom Carlos I, King of Portugal. Declining an invitation to reside in the Paço das Necessidades, the Emperor selected the Hotel Bragança as his place of residence. He never ceased hoping that he would be recalled to Brazil and always expressed the desire that such a call should come from the people. Dona Thereza Christina Maria, his wife, "Mother of the Brazilians," died on December 28, 1889, a few weeks after their arrival in Portugal.[21] Dom Pedro, the philosophical Emperor, who had loved books and learning more than government, died in the Bedford Hotel in Paris on December 5, 1891, three days after his sixty-sixth birthday.[22]

The uncertainty and doubt concerning the outcome of the November 15 revolution lingered during the following day.[23] There was constant fear of a counterrevolution among the leaders of the new government. Apprehension was expressed about the possibility that Marshal Deodoro's oldest brother, Marshal Hermes Ernesto da Fonseca, commandant of arms of the province of Bahia, who had sanctioned the overthrow of the ministry while opposing the fall of Pedro II, might come to the aid of the deposed monarch. Deodoro's inaction regarding this possibility caused alarm in the Republican camp.[24] With the departure of the imperial family, the provisional government became more secure and its leaders less apprehensive.

19. Monteiro, *Pesquisas e depoimentos* . . . , p. 276.
20. *Contribuições*, p. 895.
21. *Ibid.*, p. 900.
22. *Ibid.*, p. 916; Rocha Pombo, X, 443.
23. Mattoso, p. 41; Duque-Estrada, p. ix.
24. Rocha Pombo, X, 229.

At 3 P.M. on November 16, the officers of the new government "instituted by the people, the army and the navy" went to the Municipal House of Rio de Janeiro where there was a session of local municipal officials.[25] The officials had been informed that the members of the provisional government were to make a statement. Lieutenant Colonel João de Medeiros Mallet read the following motion to the local officials: "The events which occurred in this city yesterday should lead to the establishment of a Republic."[26] This motion was approved. Later the members of the provisional government entered the building. A large number of army and naval officers and people of all classes accompanied them. After receiving them, the president of the local government read the following statement:

On November 16, 1889, the provisional government of the Republic of Brazil composed of citizens Manoel Deodoro da Fonseca, Ruy Barbosa, Aristides da Silveira Lobo, Benjamin Constant, Quintino Bocayuva and Eduardo Wandenkolk, appeared before the Municipal Council, met in extraordinary session, and swore to maintain the peace, public liberty and the rights of citizens to respect and cause to be respected the obligations of the Nation, internally as well as in foreign countries, in accordance with which the said citizens sign with the city aldermen this promise with the people of Brazil, represented at this moment by the municipality of the city of Rio de Janeiro.[27]

Marshal Deodoro had reluctantly agreed to become the chief executive of the provisional government a few days before the revolution of November 15. When the conspirators had made the suggestion, he in turn had suggested that he be minister of war and that Benjamin Constant be president. Constant and others who had been present at the meeting had refused to sanction this plan, and Deodoro had been forced to assume the military and political leadership of the movement.[28] Thus, the first decree of the provisional government dated November 15, but published on November 16, bore his signature as president of the new government. This decree declared that the government of Brazil was a federated republic, the United States of Brazil, and authorization was given for the organization of the governments of the provinces as federal states.

The second decree of the government appointed the following men

25. Galanti, V, 188.
26. Rocha Pombo, X, 185.
27. *Ibid.*, X, 185.
28. Senna, p. 254; Monteiro, *Pesquisas e depoimentos* . . . , p. 207.

to the ministries of the provisional government: Aristides da Silveira Lobo, minister of interior; Quintino Bocayuva, minister of foreign affairs and temporarily of agriculture, commerce, and public works; Benjamin Constant, minister of war; Eduardo Wandenkolk, minister of the navy; Ruy Barbosa, minister of finance and temporarily of justice. Later the prominent Republicans Manuel Ferraz de Campos Salles and Demetrio Ribeiro were named to the posts of minister of justice and minister of agriculture, commerce, and public works, respectively.[29] When the decrees were sent to Marshal Deodoro late on the night of November 15, he did not recognize Demetrio Ribeiro's name and asked that he be identified. Glycerio, who had carried the lists to Deodoro, explained that Ribeiro was prominent in Republican circles in Rio Grande do Sul. The marshal, who was not a politician, did not concern himself further, "There I only know Castilhos, Assis Brasil and Ramiro, but there it is," and he signed the decree.[30]

Other decrees passed by the provisional government provided that all literate male Brazilians were eligible to vote and to hold public office. Provinces were declared extinct and such areas were reclassified as states, having governors instead of presidents as their executives. A decree dated November 27 declared that the authority to nominate governors of states, commanders of armies, and chiefs of police was the exclusive authority of the federal government.

The government gave immediate concern to the army, and its third decree, published on November 16, stated that in appreciation of the co-operation which the soldiers of the army had given the new regime when it was being established the enlistment service of recruits in the army was reduced to nine years and corporal punishment in the armed forces was abolished.[31] The strength of the army was raised to 24,877 officers and men. Later the Tiradentes Club, named for the Republican hero of the eighteenth century, was authorized to organize the Tiradentes Battalion for the defense of the republic.

The national flag was changed, but the colors of the imperial flag were retained. The new flag contained twenty-one stars, and in acknowledgment of Brazil's geographic position the Southern Cross was a feature of the new national standard. The influence of the philosophy of Auguste Comte was seen in the national motto which appeared on the flag, "Order and Progress." The national coat of arms and the national seal were also changed.[32]

29. Maximiliano, p. 85.
30. Monteiro, *Pesquisas e depoimentos* . . . , p. 212.
31. Fontoura Castallat, II, 37; Rocha Pombo, X, 226.
32. Rocha Pombo, X, 267.

After almost a month of careful consideration a decree was
published on January 8, 1890, which forbade the passage of laws
which would allow a state religion or which would create differences
between citizens because of their beliefs, philosophies, or religion.
Later decrees authorized civil marriage and secularization of burial.[33]

By a decree of December 3, 1889, the government appointed a
constituent committee. Committee members were Joaquim Saldanha
Marinho (president), Americo Braziliense de Almeida Mello, Antonio Luiz dos Santos Werneck, Francisco Rangel Pestana, and José
Antonio Pedreira de Magalhães Castro. A Constituent Congress
would be elected to consider the constitution which the committee
would write. On June 22, 1890, it was decreed that this Constituent
Congress would meet on November 15 of the same year.[34] The committee which had been named by the government worked on the
constitution for several months. Ruy Barbosa was assigned to the
committee when it seemed that the work was progressing too slowly.
After a portion of the work had been completed, Ruy Barbosa cus-
tomarily took it to Deodoro's home where the marshal either approved
or disapproved. Many of the proposals were altered by Deodoro,
particularly those which referred to the army and to the navy.[35]
It is reported that after the constitution had been completed it was
brought to Deodoro for his final approval. Deodoro looked at the
articles carefully and, not finding the one which he sought, asked Ruy
Barbosa, "Where is the article which authorizes the president to dissolve the congress?" When he was informed that there was no such
article, the marshal said, "Then the master will have to leave Congress
one day like Antonio Carlos in 1823, bowing his head to the majesty
of the cannon."[36]

While the project of the constitution was being considered the
marshal encountered many difficulties in his attempt to adjust himself to life as a politician and supreme head of a nation. Habit-
uated to instant obedience in his life as an army officer, he possessed
none of the tact and skill required for successfully controlling the
varied personalities who confronted him as citizens of the nation of
which he was leader. An example of his lack of tact is his sarcastic
comment to an office seeker who asked favors of him at a social func-

33. Galanti, V, 147; Assis Brasil, p. 13.
34. *Mensagens presidenciais, documentos parlamentares, 1891-1910* (Rio de
Janeiro, 1912), p. 15.
35. Aurelino Leal, *História constitucional do Brasil* (Rio de Janeiro, 1931),
pp. 212-213.
36. Leal, p. 214.

tion. The office seeker mentioned his need of aid and reminded the marshal that he had been a Republican since 1872. Deodoro informed the man that he evidently was very unlucky, because he himself had been a Republican only a few months, since November 15, 1889, and already was president of Brazil.[37]

On December 18, 1889, when the officers of the regiments of the city left their posts to bid officers of the Chilean cruiser *Almirante Cochrane* farewell, a riot occurred in the quarters of one of the regiments. Three or four soldiers were killed and many others were wounded before order was restored. The fear that royalist politicians had been seeking to influence the soldiers of that regiment aroused apprehension among the members of the government, and rigid measures were taken against the commander of the regiment that had rioted.[38] In the investigation which followed, all former members of the monarchist regime were questioned, but no connection with monarchist plots was discovered. However, this incident led the government to issue the decree of December 23, 1889, which restricted the freedom of the press. The decree provided that a tribunal of military officers would be organized to judge according to military law certain criminal cases, including "Those who advise or promote by words, writing or acts, civilian disorder or military revolts." This decree practically ended the discussion of political affairs in the press. The journals of the city obeyed the decree, but many of those accustomed to thriving on the discussion of the nation's political affairs suspended publication.[39] By limiting the freedom of the press, Marshal Deodoro deprived the country of a freedom which had been traditional throughout the empire period, and at the same time he earned for himself and for his government the hatred of many literate Brazilians.

Deodoro was aware that he possessed little administrative and political ability, and during the first month of his presidency he permitted his ministers to have unrestricted control of the policies of their offices.[40] The politicians who surrounded him were aware of his sentiments in this matter and they went so far as to suggest that matters of great importance be decided by a majority vote of a Council of Ministers.[41] The marshal agreed to this suggestion and the council was organized with his nephew, João Severiano da Fonseca

37. Senna, p. 149.
38. Galanti, V, 191.
39. Rocha Pombo, X, 271.
40. Turner, p. 104.
41. Rocha Pombo, X, 272.

Hermes, as secretary. This council began sharing the executive policy of the administration on January 2, 1890. During the next six weeks, when many of the most disputed measures of the provisional government were passed, no record of the initiators of the measures was made. It is possible than many of the disputed measures which caused the Republicans of the south to withdraw their support from the marshal were not initiated by Deodoro, but were the handiwork of some other member of the council. The decree which made Deodoro Generalíssimo of the land and sea forces was passed during this period. The discussion of secularization of marriage and burial was also initiated then.

Although Deodoro had approved the establishment of the council and the provision that no member of the council could publish or enact a decree which had not been approved by a majority of the members, he believed that he, as leader of the government, retained a certain degree of executive authority. A decree which was published January 17 concerning the issue of paper currency by the minister of finance, Ruy Barbosa, and which had the approval of Deodoro, became the source of a bitter conflict in the January 30 meeting of the council.[42] At this meeting the other members, offended by the action of the minister of finance and of the chief of the government, sought to have the decree revoked. Deodoro maintained that the decree could not be revoked and said that he would resign his office if the members insisted on such a move. After heated discussion, Demetrio Ribeiro, a Rio Grande do Sul Republican, resigned his office and became one of the principal opponents of the government. Senhor Glycerio was named to fill the office from which Ribeiro had resigned. In the face of these conflicts Deodoro was already coming to believe that the revolution had been a mistake: ''The people have not made their opinion known; the blood which did not flow on November 15, must flow.''[43]

On February 8, 1890, another minister, Aristides Lobo, resigned his office because of a conflict with Deodoro regarding some nominations which he had made. Cesario Alvim, who replaced him in office, was present at the meeting of February 15 when Benjamin Constant suggested that Deodoro become dictator and that the members of the council be relegated to the position of secretaries.[44] The council members disapproved of this proposal.

42. *Ibid.*, X, 273.
43. Monteiro, *Pesquisas e depoimentos* . . . , p. 326.
44. Rocha Pombo, X, 274.

One month later, annoyed by the censure of Cesario Alvim by Major Jayme Benevolo, and by certain articles published in *Democracia* by Captain Saturnino Cardoso, Deodoro opened the meeting of the Council of Ministers by declaring that he had pointed out these violations of regulations to the minister of war, but that no effective action had been taken. Referring to the state of discipline in the army, he further criticized the minister when he said that "the corps are abandoned by their commanders; Major Solon, for example, spends his time on the street, and never appears at the quarters, thereby sacrificing the discipline of his command."[45] He advised that the most energetic measures be taken and remarked that if Constant did not take proper steps, he would take them himself. "It is better not to have an army than to have one which lacks discipline."[46]

Immediately following this session of the council the marshal was again annoyed by the opposition which the government was receiving from the press. Dr. Pedro Taveres, a former governor of Maranhão, was imprisoned because of his criticism. Deodoro complained that such criticism was unfair and that it injured the public welfare and the free action of the government. On March 31, 1890, Campos Salles presented the famous *decreto rolha* (corking decree), which was approved by the council and which was designed to end the criticism which the government had been receiving from the press. However, it was impossible to silence the critics, and the president continued to complain about them and to insist that the ministers rigidly enforce the decrees against unfair and unjust criticism of the government.[47]

These and other irritating factors led Deodoro to become exceedingly disgusted with his position. On May 6, 1890, the marshal sent a letter to Ruy Barbosa in which he delivered to him the authority with which he had been invested. The letter indicates that Deodoro was aware of his inability to cope with the problems of administering the country.

The high office with which I have been invested is impossible for me considering that I do not have the patience of Job, nor desire the martyrdom of Jesus Christ. I consider myself without sufficient stamina to continue in such an office. Therefore, I am delivering to you as the first vice chief of the government, the powers which were conferred upon me, and I am returning to my quarters, where I will

45. *Ibid.*
46. *Ibid.*
47. Fleiuss, *História administrativa* . . . , pp. 450-451.

be found, when, in matters dealing with my profession, there is need of an old soldier.[48]

Ruy Barbosa was able to soothe the marshal's irritation and Deodoro did not resign his position.

It is possible the marshal's patience had reached this breaking point because of the controversy within his council over the campaign to drive the robbers and brawlers from the streets of Rio de Janeiro. During the second empire the capital had been infested with these robbers who had, it seemed, become an accepted institution, one which all admitted was undesirable, but at the same time one about which nothing could be done. The influence and relationships of the thieves sometimes reached into the highest circles and into the best families of the city. Consequently, because of fear of injury to prominent families or of incurring the wrath of important people, little effort had been made to eradicate the evil, and the streets of the city were the scenes of nightly robberies and brawls.

Two months after the inauguration of the provisional government, Marshal Deodoro took steps to end this menace to life and property. Sampaio Ferraz, chief of police of Rio de Janeiro, was ordered to take rigid measures to exterminate the robbers. On receipt of this order, Ferraz warned Deodoro that its execution would involve conflict with persons high in military and political circles, since the leaders of the robbers were in many instances members of influential families or had friends who were influential in governmental circles.[49] Despite this warning, Deodoro informed the chief of police that he would give him the full support of the government and that he desired the strongest measures to be taken against the bandits.

The agents of the chief of police knew most of the bandits, and Ferraz quickly began his campaign to end the robberies. The bandit leaders were arrested and confined in the city jail where they were severely dealt with. After confinement and trial they were sent to the far northern insular fort of Fernando de Noronha, where they were required to serve sentences at hard labor.[50] As the police officer had predicted, these measures quickly had their repercussions in political circles. One of the bandits, José Elysio dos Reis, was a brother of Count Mattosinhos, owner of *Paiz*, a newspaper which was edited by Quintino Bocayuva, minister of foreign affairs. The count obtained

48. Rocha Pombo, X, 275.
49. Galanti, V, 152.
50. *Ibid.*, V, 157.

a promise from Bocayuva that his brother would be released. However, Deodoro permitted no distinction to be made, and he insisted that José Elysio suffer the same penalty as the other bandits. At the meeting of the Council of Ministers, April 10, 1890, Bocayuva demanded that José Elysio be released and threatened to resign his office unless this was done.[51] The position taken by Bocayuva was an irritating factor within the council, and at the meeting of April 12 Campos Salles said that if José Elysio did not suffer a fate similar to that of the other thieves he would resign his office. Campos Salles told the members of the council that he knew the story of the youth's life and that the boy had always been a source of shame to his family. On April 19, Bocayuva admitted that the position taken by the other councilors was just and correct, but he said that his honor required that he resign his post in the government. Deodoro insisted that he retain his post and promised that the minister of war would make an explanation of the matter to the Reis family; however, he did not for one instant consider making special concessions in favor of the imprisoned youth.[52]

Trained through long years of practice to follow army regulations and not gifted with the facile ability of the *politico* to yield when circumstances seem unfavorable, Deodoro continued to be confronted with problems which demanded patience and tactful judgment. In most situations the marshal failed to demonstrate that he possessed these essential traits. For instance, the Ministry of Public Instructions, Mails, and Telegraph had not been created in answer to a need for such a ministry, but it had been a skilful means to remove Benjamin Constant from the post of minister of war.[53] Constant had permitted himself to be influenced by a group of young officers to the extent that the discipline and training of the army had been neglected. The irritation created by this situation caused antagonism between the two founders of the republic and displayed itself in a disagreeable manner at the meeting of the council in the palace at Itamaraty on September 27, 1890.[54] A nomination which Deodoro had made for treasurer of the postal system of the state of Rio Grande do Norte had been ignored by Constant, who at this time was minister of public instructions, mails, and telegraph. He had named a person to occupy the office, and rather than have that man dismissed, as

51. Rocha Pombo, X, 277.
52. Galanti, V, 157.
53. Lyra, p. 287.
54. Galanti, V, 164.

Deodoro demanded, he preferred to resign. Constant accused Deodoro of creating a conflict over this issue, when the cause of his anger lay elsewhere. The enraged Deodoro told Constant that since both of them were military men they could decide the issue with their swords, and he seemed prepared to throw himself upon Constant. Two ministers intervened and Floriano Peixoto led Constant to another room while Campos Salles conducted Deodoro to a private apartment where the president suffered a serious heart attack. Constant, who was almost the same age as Deodoro, also suffered a heart attack, and it is reported that he never recovered from the effects of this incident. All efforts were made to suppress accounts of this unfortunate encounter between the founders of the republic, but the news spread rapidly and had an adverse effect upon the spirit of the people of Rio de Janeiro and of Brazil.[55]

In his endeavor to play the part in which he had been cast, Deodoro sought to have the ministry agree to make important alterations in the sanitary system of Rio de Janeiro. He proposed that the harbors of Rio Grande do Norte, Sergipe, Rio Grande do Sul, and other states of Brazil be improved. He seemed genuinely interested in bettering the economic conditions of the country. The other ministers, looking upon him as a figurehead and giving little consideration to his proposals, found plausible reasons to prohibit such projects from being carried out. A repeated series of these objections made Deodoro realize that the ministers had never given serious consideration to his proposals, and he felt that they had been treating him like a simpleton.[56]

The press continued its attacks upon the government despite the ''corking decree'' and despite Deodoro's complaints that the journals were creating false issues in order to discredit the administration. The *Gazeta de Noticias*, the *Cidade do Rio*, and especially the *Tribuna*, a monarchist organ, made frequent attacks upon the government. Many of the higher army officers sympathized with the marshal's complaints about the press, and in November when a rumor reached Campos Salles, the minister of justice, that some officers planned a physical attack on the *Tribuna*, he sought out Deodoro and reported it to him. Deodoro ridiculed the rumor and assured the minister that nothing would come of it. Deodoro was mistaken; the press of that newspaper was attacked and damaged, and one of the employees who

55. Rocha Pombo, X, 281.
56. ''Sôbre o saneamento da Capital Federal,'' *RIHGB*, LXXII, Pt. 2, 144.

was slow in fleeing from the building was killed.[57] This incident aroused public indignation, and on the day following the attack six ministers submitted their resignations to the president. Deodoro refused to accept the resignations, and at the meeting of the council on December 1, 1890, Glycerio said that the ministry should dismiss itself and that those who were responsible for the assault on the newspaper and for the murder of its employee should be severely punished. Deodoro, while refusing to accept the resignation of the ministers, informed them that he would give them complete freedom to deal with the perpetrators of the crime. He added, however, that if the ministers insisted upon resigning their offices, he too would resign his post. Confronted with the prospect of Deodoro's resignation and the disorder which might result from such an act, the ministers decided to retain their places in the government. Deodoro then reminded them of his efforts to have the laws against the press enforced and to have suitable new measures passed designed to limit attacks upon the government. His suggestions had been ignored, whereas the ministers had dealt satisfactorily with other problems of lesser importance.

During the next meetings of the council there was discussion of a press law, but it never passed the discussion stage. From the meeting on December 1, 1890, to the last meeting of the council on January 17, 1891, the sessions were infrequent and practically nothing was done by the council. The last meeting of the council, that of January 17, has been described by one Brazilian historian as "terrible."[58]

Deodoro, still attempting to advance his program of construction of ports and improvement of public utilities in Rio de Janeiro, had awarded the rights for the construction of the port of Torres in Rio Grande do Sul to a personal friend. The minister of the interior, who was absent, stated in a letter to the council that he opposed the measure, not because it would not be beneficial to the country, but because the time was inopportune. The other ministers agreed with him. Deodoro was angered because the ministers, who had not hesitated to hand over hundreds of contracts to their own personal friends, sought in this manner to block his effort to aid a friend; he said that he would sign no more measures until such time as his project was approved.[59] The ministers attempted to have the measure

57. Rocha Pombo, X, 284.
58. Galanti, V, 168.
59. Calmon, *História Social do Brasil*, III, 23.

considered by the Constituent Congress, but Deodoro did not relent. Since the Constitution had been completed and had passed its first reading in the legislature, the ministers decided to resign their posts. On January 20, 1891, they met in one of the rooms of the Quintada Boa Vista, or Palácio São Chistovão, and after a brief discussion submitted their resignations to Deodoro.[60] Floriano Peixoto, minister of war, at that time was at his home in Palmeiras because of illness, but he sanctioned the move made by his colleagues. On January 21, Deodoro accepted the resignations of the ministers and organized a new ministry which was dominated by his friend Baron Lucena.[61]

The Constitution, approved by the congress on February 24, 1891, was the supreme law of the land for the United States of Brazil. In it the nation was described as a federal republic. Its executive department included a president and a vice-president who were to be elected for four-year terms by the people by absolute majority vote. Cabinet offices and secretaries were to be appointed by the president. The legislative department included a Senate and a House of Deputies. Three senators from each state were elected by the people to serve terms of nine years. Deputies were elected to serve terms of three years, and representation in the lower house was based on population of the states. The judicial department provided a federal court system. The Supreme Court was to have fifteen judges, and such subordinate courts as were needed were to be established by act of the legislature. Literate males twenty-one and over were granted the franchise. This Constitution permitted freedom of worship and had a Bill of Rights similar to that of the United States.

On the night of the promulgation of the Constitution, copy of the proof of the *Diário Oficial* appeared on the streets containing the statement that by a decree "the Provisional Government sanctioned the Constitution." Dr. Lopes Travao, after having seen this proof, went to the palace at Itamaraty and pointed out to Deodoro the absurdity of this statement. The marshal had the presses of the *Diário Oficial* stopped, and the announcement of the promulgation of the Constitution had no reference to the sanction of the president of the provisional government.[62]

The first thing to be considered after the promulgation of the Constitution was the election of a president and vice-president, a

60. *Ibid.*, III, 24; Oscar d'Araujo, "Le fondateur de la republique brésilienne, Benjamin Constant Botelho de Magalhães," *La Nouvelle Revue*, LXXI, 475.

61. Monteiro, *Pesquisas e depoímentos . . .* , p. 329; Fleiuss, *História administrativa . . .* , p. 434.

62. Rocha Pombo, X, 336.

task which fell to the Constituent Congress. Deodoro's ineptness as a politician had made many enemies for the hero of November 15. In addition, there remained the civilian politicians' suspicion and distrust of the military. The *políticos*, who had so consistently sought the military while they were endeavoring to prevent the third reign and to establish the republic, now wished to cast aside the man who had been their instrument. They sought to convince the electorate that it was detrimental to the country to have a military man as its chief executive.

The most influential opponents of the marshal sponsored the candidacy of Prudente de Moraes, the man who had been president of the constituent assembly; to counter the influence of Deodoro with the army, Floriano Peixoto was named as their candidate for vice-president. Prominent among the sponsors of the candidacy of these men were General José Simeão, a senator from Pernambuco; Rear Admiral Custodio de Mello, a deputy from Bahia; and Dr. Demetrio Ribeiro, a former minister of agriculture and now a deputy from Rio Grande do Sul.[63] Senator Simeão had been removed from the governorship of Pernambuco by Marshal Deodoro. Rear Admiral de Mello was a personal enemy of the Fonseca family, and in addition he was the leader of a group of jealous naval officers who looked with envy upon the spoils which had come to the army as a result of its victory of November 15, 1889. Demetrio Ribeiro was the Republican who in anger had resigned his office because of Deodoro's refusal to sanction a nomination which he had made. "It was thus that individual feelings and ambitions of local politicians guided the opposition which sought thereby, to obtain the sympathy of the nation by pretending to base their opposition to the marshal on the basis of war against militarism."[64]

Campos Salles called a meeting of his friends and attempted to convince them that it would be better for the republic if Deodoro were elected. He suggested that Deodoro's candidacy be indorsed and that the indorsement be made known to the people. Campos Salles argued that since the states were not yet organized, any grave disorder could have the most unfortunate consequences for the republic. If Prudente de Moraes won the election, the army would be certain to revolt and there would be a repetition of the events of November 15.[65] Although Deodoro had lost the friendship of many of the *políticos* and

63. *Ibid.*, X, 337.
64. *Ibid.*, X, 338.
65. Maximiliano, p. 93.

his prestige with the people had declined, his popularity with the troops remained. Glycerio and others who had met with Campos Salles agreed with his suggestion, and arrangements were made to have Prudente de Moraes nominated for the vice-presidency. General José Simeano and two companions refused to agree with this proposal, and since Prudente would not withdraw his candidacy for the presidency, the meeting then had to be considered a failure. So certain were the politicians of Deodoro's inability to win without their indorsement that the election of Prudente de Moraes was considered almost a foregone conclusion.[66]

Since rumors were circulating that the army would not stand idly by should Deodoro fail to be elected president, Campos Salles consulted with Floriano Peixoto and José Simeão about the defense of the Constituent Congress should it be attacked by the troops after the election. At the meeting in Simeão's on February 24, 1891, Campos Salles, Floriano Peixoto, Simeão, and General Osorio, a deputy from Rio Grande do Sul, decided that should the congress be attacked Prudente would be given immediate possession of the office and that without delay the constitutional government would be installed within the building.[67] After this the members of the new government and the congress would await further developments. The two generals were expected to contact troops on whom the congress could depend, and they were to direct the defense plans of the congress. Marshal Floriano did not hide his apprehension that such measures would be of little avail if the troops revolted because of the failure of the congress to name Deodoro as president of the republic.[68]

On February 25, 1891, the Constituent Congress cast votes for the presidency of the republic. The election was conducted in an atmosphere of apprehension, but those who had feared that the election of Prudente de Moraes would cause a revolution saw their fears dispelled in a most disagreeable manner. Marshal Deodoro, instead, was elected. Many of those who had been the most outspoken in their opposition to his candidacy cast their votes for him. Marshal Floriano Peixoto was elected to the vice-presidency.

When the two marshals were summoned to the chamber in which the congress was meeting, Deodoro's entrance was greeted with the

66. Calmon, *História Social do Brasil*, III, 29.
67. Rocha Pombo, X, 338.
68. *Ibid.*, X, 339.

coldest of silences, but that of Floriano drew loud *vivas*.[69] Thus, the stage was set for the conflict which was to develop between the executive and legislative branches of the government. "The Congress and the President of the Republic looked at each other at this first meeting as adversaries scrutinize each other in the arena."[70]

The president of the republic was confronted by this legislative opposition until the time of his resignation from office. After the election, all of the states whose representatives had opposed the candidacy of Deodoro had an almost complete change in their political personnel. The scenes which had been common during the empire period, when the victorious party frequently removed defeated party members from the ministry and replaced them with members of its party, were now re-enacted. This use of the spoils system provoked deep irritation within the states, and the resentment which the members of the congress carried to their home states did much to discredit the new government.

The first regular session of the federal Congress opened on July 15, 1891. The antagonism which had existed between the executive and legislative powers continued. Each viewed the other with suspicion and it seemed impossible to establish an accord between them. Such a conflict between the two powers indicated that little would be accomplished of benefit to Brazil. In the first months of the legislative session, Deodoro and Marshal Floriano were the victims of frequent illness. During their absence Prudente de Moraes was elected to the presidency of the Senate. The illness of the two highest officers of the government caused Campos Salles, one of the few politicians who seemed more concerned about the welfare of Brazil than about personal grandeur, to seek to modify the president's cabinet to the extent that two or three of the Historical Republicans (men who had sponsored the establishment of a republic in Brazil since the 1870's) would be placed in it so that the executive part of the government could gain some support among the members of the Congress.[71] It was hoped that this move would establish an accord between the two powers, but nothing came of it.

At the conferences wherein the opposition leaders sought an accord with the executive power, Luceana had asked that two laws which were being considered by the legislature be withdrawn. Both of the proposed acts were unconstitutional. One of the proposed acts

69. Calmon, *História Social do Brasil*, III, 30.
70. Galanti, V, 173.
71. Monteiro, *Pesquisas e depoimentos . . .* , p. 330.

would have given civil marriages precedence over the religious ceremony, and the second would have prohibited the wearing of decorations and the use of titles.[72] This second measure aroused anger
among the soldiers who saw themselves in danger of being deprived
of the decorations which they had won on the field of battle. The
troops of the Rio de Janeiro garrison had decided to demonstrate
before the legislators in protest against the proposed law by carrying
the insignias and decorations which they had won during the Paraguayan War. Deodoro learned of their plot and ordered them to
make no such demonstration. But this did not settle the question in
the barracks where the more radical of the soldiers spoke of demonstrating "without the old man's knowing about it."[73]

Prudente's answer to this opposition to the laws was to place
them on the agenda for immediate consideration. Marshal Deodoro,
seeking to quiet the anger of the troops, appeared before the Congress
without his medals and decorations. This unfortunate situation did
not improve, and when the House of Deputies elected as its president
Barnardino de Campos, one of the most passionate opponents of
the executive power, it became obvious that Deodoro was without
friends in the legislative halls. He then began to give the most serious
thought to dissolving the legislative bodies.[74]

While the disorder and conflict within the government mounted,
the health of Marshal Deodoro became a source of the deepest concern. During September, 1891, the marshal passed three days in a
coma, and his physician, Dr. Marinho, told Lucena that he might die
at any moment. Every effort was made to suppress the information
concerning the seriousness of his condition, but the news became
known. Civilian politicians who had sought to use Marshal Floriano
during the campaign for the presidency in February now searched
for means to deprive him of the presidency should Deodoro die. One
such politician approached Lucena and sought his support, informing him that he had already done some work in the quarters.[75] When
Lucena inquired about the solution whereby the *politico* would evade
the constitutional provision for Floriano's succession, he was told
that Quintino Bocayuva would be selected and that the states would
dictate the laws of the republic.

Floriano was aware of the condition of Deodoro's health, and his

72. *Ibid.*
73. *Ibid.*, p. 331.
74. Galanti, V, 175.
75. Monteiro, *Pesquisas e depoimentos* . . . , p. 331.

friend in the Senate, Pires Ferreira, informed him of the plots to deprive him of the succession to the presidency. Floriano sent his friend to interview Lucena, and Lucena told the senator that he favored constitutional succession and that he opposed any effort to incite the troops to intervention in the government. Deodoro's subsequent recovery put an end to all this activity, but it had now become obvious that there were very few men of great political ability and integrity in the legislative chambers.

During October Baron Lucena began to fear that either the president would be deposed or the Congress dissolved; he suggested to Deodoro that he seek out Marshal Floriano, whose frequent illness had prevented his presiding in the Senate, and have him take his rightful place as president of the Senate, thereby removing from that important post Prudente de Moraes, inflexible foe of the executive.[76] After carefully considering the suggestion, Deodoro advised Lucena not to make the attempt:

You do not know Floriano Peixoto. I would not say that he is a coward, that would be doing an injustice to him, but he is a man gifted of a total passive nature, and has collective courage. He fulfills his duty in a creditable manner. However, he has not individual courage, I am certain of that. If he were to understand the urgency with which we need his support, he would throw himself openly into the arms of the opposition.[77]

Lucena sought to convince Deodoro that even with a marshal at its head the opposition could not defeat the government, but Deodoro was no longer considering his words. The intolerable situation in which he found himself strained his patience. Turning to his friend and aide he informed him that he could no longer tolerate the Congress, which "disregards the happiness of Brazil" and which also was refusing to pass laws authorizing the expenditure of funds for the operation of the government.[78] Deodoro ordered the baron to prepare the decree which would dissolve the Congress and not to worry about Floriano. But Lucena sought to persuade Deodoro to use moderation, and he asked him to get the opinion, and if possible, the support of Floriano. Finally, Deodoro requested that he go to Floriano and speak frankly to him of the matter.

Thus, on November 1, 1891, Lucena called upon the marshal in his home. Floriano agreed that Deodoro had just cause to be annoyed

76. *Ibid.*, p. 336.
77. *Ibid.*
78. *Ibid.*, p. 337.

with the Congress and expressed himself as being in accord with Deodoro. However, when Lucena reminded him that it was reported that he was a leader of the conspiracy, Floriano denied such reports. ''He only permitted the opponents of the government to meet in his home so that he could advise them to moderation and tolerance and so that others less prudent and dutiful have no opportunity to misguide them.''[79] Convinced that Floriano was a friend to the executive, Lucena told him that should Prudente de Moraes place before the Congress the proposed law against crime of responsibility, which was unconstitutional and which was designed to curtail the powers of the president, then Deodoro would dissolve the Congress. Should Floriano take his rightful place in the Senate, he could prevent the law from being placed before the body and thereby remove the necessity of dissolving the Congress. Floriano reminded Lucena that he was too ill to go into the streets, but he promised to use his influence in the Senate to prevent the enactment of the measure: ''I have not been a friend of the marshal since the day on which he doubted my loyalty, but I am his comrade, I am a soldier, and above all I am a Brazilian. You may assure the general that he will always have me at his side in whatever emergency that develops.''[80]

Despite these pledges of support, Floriano had no intention of aiding Deodoro, and at the time of making them he was conspiring against the president. Deodoro understood his old comrade, and when Lucena reported to him about the cheering results of the meeting and the promises which he received from Floriano, Deodoro's only response was ''We shall see.''[81] Six days later Lucena admitted that the conference with Floriano had been an error; he had not won the support of Floriano, and the opposition had been encouraged by it.

Meanwhile, rumors were current in Rio de Janeiro that Dom Augusto Leopoldo, son of Dom Pedro II's daughter Princess Leopoldina, had embarked on an Austrian warship which would visit Bahia and Rio de Janeiro. The Royalists of Brazil looked on this as a possible attempt by a member of the dynasty to regain the throne of Brazil and they sought to rally support for Dom Augusto.[82]

This was the confusing situation which existed in Brazil on November 3, 1891, when Marshal Deodoro had the doors of the legis-

79. *Ibid.*, p. 339.
80. Fleiuss, *História administrativa* . . . , p. 467.
81. Monteiro, *Pesquisas e depoimentos* . . . , p. 343.
82. *Ibid.*

lative halls closed to the members of Congress and thereby caused the dissolution of that body. The decree stated that the president, in order to save republican institutions, had assumed the responsibility for the dissolution of the Congress. The move, the decree stated, had been taken for the good of the country. On November 15, 1889, the monarchy had been deposed, and on November 3, 1891, Deodoro asserted that he was deposing anarchy. He also referred to the possibility that monarchists were seeking to restore the Bragança dynasty. The financial condition of the government was deplorable. Although the treasury contained ample funds for maintenance of the government, Brazil was bankrupt in the eyes of foreign states because the Congress had refused to pass laws for the expenditure of these funds. Deodoro promised to protect republican institutions during the period of his dictatorship, to govern in accordance with the Constitution, and, when opportunity presented itself, to convoke another Congress.[83]

Deodoro and his adviser had not expected any strong opposition to the act which had dissolved the Congress, and from the majority of the states telegrams poured into Rio de Janeiro containing messages of agreement with his decree. Governors, military garrisons, politicians, and others who played an active part in public life warmly indorsed the action which created military dictatorship in Brazil. "The governor of one state felt the majesty of the dictator's power to be so great that he signed his telegram as *your subject*."[84] One governor, however, Lauro Sodré of Pará, did not support the president, and his message was that "he would know how to do his duty, defending the Constitution and the Republic."[85]

The government, anticipating some statement from the opposition, declared Rio de Janeiro and its environs in a state of seige. The halls of the legislative chambers were barred to the members after publication of the dissolution decree. The members of the Congress, however, despite police vigilance, met in various groups and discussed countermeasures. There had been ample warning that such a move might take place, but the warning had not been heeded by the members of the legislature. Now the members of the Congress who had not adhered to the executive policies were invited to sign a manifesto which was to be published in all the states of Brazil. Meanwhile, congressmen returning to their home states sought to provoke

83. Fleiuss, *História administrativa* . . . , p. 466; Maximiliano, p. 13.
84. Monteiro, *Pesquisas e depoimentos* . . . , p. 325.
85. *Ibid.*, p. 345.

dissatisfaction with the government of the dictator. In São Paulo, Campos Salles edited an anti-government manifesto which was offered for sale in *Correio Paulistano* on November 9. The agents of the police seized all copies of the paper, even though the state of siege had not been extended to the city of São Paulo.[86]

The opposition, however, was making rapid headway in its effort to arouse powerful forces against Deodoro. These opponents, working skilfully in the capital and in the states, secured the adhesion of some of the most influential men in Brazil. Floriano Peixoto, José Simeão, Custodio de Mello, and Admiral Wandenkolk deserted the old marshal. The first two sought to destroy Deodoro's influence with the army, and the latter pair attempted to influence the officers of the navy. This last assignment was not difficult, for the situation promised an opportunity for the navy to secure a more influential position than it had won through its participation in the revolt of November 15.

In Rio Grande do Sul where Julio de Castilhos, a friend of Deodoro, was governor, disorder had prevailed for a long time because of the conflict between local political leaders and because of the influence of the friends of Gaspar Silveira Martins, who had been exiled by Deodoro after the fall of the monarch. Here national guard troops who had revolted in strong numbers attempted to march overland to Rio de Janeiro to overthrow Deodoro's dictatorship. Americo Brasiliense, who had remained faithful to the marshal, was deposed from the office of governor of São Paulo by the people of that city.[87] In Pará where the discontented Lauro Sodré governed, the Senate of the state "regretted the act of the president of the republic and condemned it."

Deodoro, grimly hanging on to the reins of government despite his poor health, made plans for an elaborate celebration of the second anniversary of the establishment of the republic. Lucena was sent to Marshal Floriano's home with a letter requesting that the marshal take charge of the military activities on the day of festivities. One of Floriano's daughters informed Lucena that her father was not at home, and the letter was left for him. No reply was received until November 15 when Deodoro was making last-minute preparations for the event. That morning an officer came to the presidential palace and informed Deodoro that Floriano could not participate because "the

86. Rocha Pombo, X, 342.
87. Fleiuss, *História administrativa* . . . , p. 467.

uniform which he had was not suitable for the occasion."[88] The old comrade had not been respectful enough to send a letter; the message was delivered vocally.

To this bit of handwriting on the wall was added the refusal of Lauro Muller, governor of Santa Catharina and a personal friend of Deodoro, to oppose the advance of the rebel national guard troops from Rio Grande do Sul. In Rio de Janeiro itself, the influence of the military who were working with the conspirators was felt. The troops and naval units of the federal district were passing over to the side of Deodoro's opponents.

Until the day before the revolution, Deodoro was confident that the military would not desert him, and he felt so secure that he assured Lucena, who tried to warn him of the dangers which confronted the government, that "No one would dare step out of line."[89] But learning of the conspiracy on Sunday, November 22, Deodoro ordered the imprisonment of Quintino Bocayuva and Admiral Wandenkolk. However, difficulties were experienced in securing transportation because of a strike of the transit workers. At midnight on that day Deodoro suffered a severe heart attack and afterwards fell into a restless sleep. His health had been very poor all during the spring months, and at the celebration on November 15 he had needed assistance in mounting his horse, which he insisted on riding to defy would-be monarchist assassins who were reported to have arrived from Paris to kill him.[90]

While the marshal slept, Admiral Saldanha da Gama, one of the loyal naval officers, telephoned requesting authorization to use two battalions of infantry to recapture a warship which had rebelled. Lucena transmitted the order to Frota, minister of war, but that minister refused to obey the order and said that he would take orders only from the president of the republic. Because of the condition of Deodoro's health, Lucena would not wake him so that the order might be given. At 6 A.M. when Deodoro learned of da Gama's request, he immediately gave the necessary commands. He also gave orders for the troops in all of the fortresses and on the Ilha das Cobras to resist the attacks of the revolutionary forces. Then the brave old soldier took out a revolver and prepared it for action. "They will only enter here over my dead body," he said.[91]

88. Monteiro, *Pesquisas e depoimentos* . . . , p. 346.
89. Rocha Pombo, X, 369.
90. *Ibid.*, X, 361.
91. *Ibid.; Humberto de Campos, O Brasil Anedótico* (Rio de Janeiro, 1941), p. 21.

Later, Lucena told how this scene affected him. He confessed that it saddened him to see Deodoro, who had one life-and-death struggle taking place in his own body, preparing to participate in this new combat. Later that morning Deodoro reconsidered, and thinking that the rebels might advance to the north to effect a juncture with Dom Augusto and to seek to restore the monarchy, he decided to resign his office. He thought that Brazil would be spared a bloody civil war and that republican institutions would be saved if he resigned. He reminded Lucena that at the time of the dissolution of Congress they had considered including his resignation in the decree, and he requested that Lucena prepare such a decree of resignation now. Deodoro then directed his aides to call Admiral Saldanha and ask him to make no further resistance. Orders were given for a carriage to be sent to Marshal Floriano so that he could come to talk with Deodoro. Turning to those who were present, Deodoro said, "I am no longer president of the Republic, and I am going to ask that I be retired from the army."[92]

The military commanders who were present protested against Deodoro's action and begged him to reconsider. But the decision remained unchanged. Colonel Lobo Botelho, when he arrived at Floriano's home, found the vice-president at breakfast and was informed by Floriano that he had been "awaiting Manoel's decision." On receipt of Deodoro's message the vice-president went to the presidential palace immediately and conferred with him. Deodoro submitted to Floriano his resignation from the presidency and from the army. Baron Lucena expressed a desire to go to the treasury building to get some papers, but the new president advised, "Don't go, do not expose yourself." In a message to the people of Brazil Deodoro said:

The conditions in which during the last days the country finds itself, the ingratitude of those for whom I have sacrificed so much, and the desire not to permit a civil war in my homeland cause me to place the powers of the government in the hands of the person who replaces me. I pray to the Almighty for the perpetual prosperity and ever increasing advancement of my beloved Brazil.[93]

On November 24, 1891, Deodoro retired to a house which he had purchased on the Rua do Riachuelo. Disgusted with the betrayal of those whom he had trusted, he placed all of his military decorations

92. Monteiro, *Pesquisas e depoimentos* . . . , p. 363.
93. Fleiuss, *História administrativa* . . . , p. 463; "Marechal Manoel Deodoro da Fonseca," *RIHGB*, LV, Pt. 2, 536.

and medals in a large container and ordered that they be thrown into the sea. His fall from leadership of the government coincided with a decline in his health. Throughout the remainder of his days the marshal was angered at the treatment which Floriano's regime accorded those who had supported him on November 23, 1891, for Floriano removed all of the governors appointed by Deodoro, with the exception of Lauro Sodré, and all political offices were filled by men who were supporters of the new regime.

In January, 1892, a revolt led by Sergeant Silvino de Macedo with the intent of restoring Deodoro to the presidency was defeated by government forces. In March, when the health of the marshal was a cause of grave concern to his friends and relatives, thirteen general officers submitted a manifesto to Floriano. The manifesto suggested that a new president be elected before Deodoro's elected term expired. As a result of this attempt to force Floriano to adhere to the Constitution, eleven of the officers were retired and two of them were demoted in rank. At the same time a demonstration in front of Deodoro's home led to the arrest of many civilians and military officers and to the imprisonment and deportation of several officers. Among those suffering such penalties were several who had played prominent parts in the revolution of November 15, 1889: General Almeida Barreto, Colonel Antonio Adolpho da Fontoura Menna Barreto, Jacques Ourique, Admiral Wandenkolk, Sebastião Bandeira, and José do Patrocinio.[94]

In April the marshal was advised by his physician to move to Petrópolis. From that city he wrote to Floriano protesting against the actions which the new president had taken against the old comrades. His position as a threat to Floriano was not an effective one, for in April after the punishment of the general officers Deodoro underwent a mental and physical decline which was to prove fatal. He suffered hallucinations and his mind was no longer sound. There were times when he thought that he was again faced with the crisis of November 23. In the voice of a commanding general he would demand, ''Where is the infantry which does not march? Where is the cavalry which does not advance?'' Then, perhaps realizing his condition, he would say, ''I must write a letter to Floriano and to Mello telling them that they are the most powerful in the land and that they do things which I had not the courage nor the power to do.''[95]

After one of these attacks in April, 1892, Deodoro lost the power

94. Fleiuss, *História administrativa* . . . , p. 484.
95. Monteiro, *Pesquisas e depoímentos* . . . , p. 365.

of speech. This condition endured until the day of his death, August 22, 1892, at the age of sixty-five. In accordance with his desire, he was buried in civilian clothing, without the military honors which his service to Brazil merited. Despite his wish, the funeral procession was halted for a few moments in front of the headquarters building where an orator spoke of his deeds on November 15, 1889: "Thus ended the man whom Cotegipe had predicted would become the new Caxias. In that role he would have maintained Conservative leadership of the military. But the 'new Caxias' had sacrificed that party, his respect for the emperor, his health and finally his life."[96]

Marshal Deodoro's greatest contribution to his country was his assumption of responsibility during the last days of the empire and his undertaking of the leading role in the establishment of the republic. Deodoro had not eagerly accepted the presidency; in fact, perhaps aware that he did not have the tact or the political skill requisite for that position, he had suggested that he become the minister of war in the provisional government. And before this occurred he had demonstrated great reluctance in the matter of proclaiming the republic. He assented only after Republican leaders emphasized the necessity of the proclamation if his beloved military class was to retain its accustomed place in Brazilian society. This reluctant president was forced by his opponents to assume reluctantly yet another role—that of dictator. And when confronted with the choice of relinquishing the presidency or becoming the center of a bloody revolution, he resigned his office and sought obscurity.

Without the aid of Marshal Deodoro the republic could not have come into existence so soon. The Republicans of Brazil in 1889 were only a clever, outspoken minority. During those crucial days when the monarchist parties seemed benumbed with inertia, this party skilfully ingratiated itself to the suspicious, neglected, and disgruntled military class. Even within the army, there remained enough supporters of the monarchy to have prevented the fall of Dom Pedro, had the Republicans not been granted the support of the most influential of Brazil's military leaders, Deodoro da Fonseca.

The success of the Republican strategy is seen in the events of November 15, 1889. Following this, the misfit alliance between Deodoro and the Republicans steadily waned. Deodoro, as provisional president and later as president of the republic, was a man of purely military training. He was accustomed to the routine of the soldier's life and lacked the basic qualifications for the position of chief

96. *Ibid.*, p. 366.

executive of the nation. The "practical men" of the Republican party realized this, and they had only sought the aid of the military to overthrow the monarchy. Once this had been accomplished, Prudente de Moraes, Campos Salles, Quintino Bocayuva, and other civilian Republicans were so anxious to obtain control of the government that they preferred, it seems, anarchy to successful government by a military leader. The conflicts within the government during the first years of the republic were not the result of dictatorial policies, but rather of the efforts of civilian political leaders to control the government.

A. *Documents and Archives*

Barbosa, Ruy. *Protecto N. 48, Sessão de 4 de Agôsto de 1884, Parecer N. 48A.* Rio de Janeiro, 1884.

Discussão da reforma do estado servil no câmara dos deputados e no senado, 1871. Rio de Janeiro, 1824.

"Documentos referentes à infância e a educação do D. Pedro II e suas irmãs." *Publicações do Arquivo Nacional,* XVII. Commodore Frederico Schumann, Director.

"Documentos sobre a questão religiosa," *Publicações do Arquivo Nacional,* XXIV. João Aleides Bezerra Cavalcanti, Director.

Mensagens presidenciais, documentos parliamentares, 1891-1910. Rio de Janeiro, 1912.

Papers Relating to the Foreign Relations of the United States. Washington, D. C., 1870.

"Quebra kilso," *Publicações do Arquivo Nacional,* XXIV. João Aleides Bezerra Cavalcanti, Director.

B. *Published Material*

Agassiz, Professor and Mrs. Louis. *A Journey in Brazil.* Boston, 1875.

Albuquerque, Madeiro E. *Quando eu era viva . . . Memórias, 1867 a 1934.* Porto Alegre, 1942.

Affonso Celso, Count de; *See* Ouro Preto, Viscount de.

Alencostre, Alvaro de. "O 7 de Abril e o exército," *Segundo Congresso da História Nacional* (Boletim do Instituto Histórico), V (1946), 253-271.

Amaral, Braz do. "O imperador e a proclamação da república," *Revista do Instituto Histórico e Geográfico Brasileiro,* CLII, 455-481.

Andrade, Maria G. L. de. *História do Brasil.* Rio de Janeiro, 1888.

Araujo, Oscar de. "Le fondateur de la république brésilienne, Benjamin Constant Botelho de Magalhaes," *La Nouvelle Revue,* LXXI, 466-477.

———. "La situation Brésilienne," *La Nouvelle Revue,* LXXIV, 807-820.

Araujo Pinho, José Wanderley de. "Pedro II e Cotegipe," *Revista do Instituto Histórico e Geográfico Brasileiro,* CLII, 479-493.

———. "A politica no império—homens e factos," *Revista do Instituto Histórico e Geográfico Brasileiro,* CLX, 59-76.

Assis Brasil, J. F. de. *Do governo presidencial na república brasileiro.* Lisbon, 1896.

164   [Marshal Deodoro and the Fall of Dom Pedro II]

Azevedo, Fernando de. *A cultura brasileira.* 2nd ed.: São Paulo, 1944.
Barbosa, Ruy. *Collectanea literária, 1868-1922.* Rio de Janeiro, 1924.
———. *Finanças e politica da república.* Rio de Janeiro, 1892.
———. "Restituições históricas," *Revista do Instituto Histórico e Geográfico Brasileiro,* LXXIII, Pt. 2, 140-145.
Barros Lins, Ivan Monteiro de. *Benjamin Constant, 1836-1891.* Rio de Janeiro, 1936.
Barroso, Gustavo. *História militar do Brasil.* 2nd ed.: São Paulo, 1938.
———. *História secreta do Brasil.* 3 vols. Rio de Janeiro, 1938.
Bennet, Frank. *Forty Years in Brazil.* London, 1914.
Besouchat, Lidia. *Mauá y su epoca.* Buenos Aires, 1940.
Box, Pelham H. "Origins of the Paraguayan War." Unpublished Ph.D. dissertation, University of Illinois, 1927.
Bruce, George J. *Brazil and the Brazilians.* New York, 1914.
Burke, Ulrick Ralph. *Business and Pleasure in Brazil.* New York, 1884.
Calcott, Maria Dundos Graham. *Journal of a Voyage to Brazil.* London, 1824.
Calmon, Pedro. *História da civilisação brasileira.* 3 vols. São Paulo, 1933.
———. *História social do Brasil.* 3 vols. 2nd ed.: São Paulo, 1940.
Calogeras, João Pandia. *A History of Brazil.* Translated and edited by Percy Alvin Martin. Chapel Hill, N. C., 1939.
Campos, Humberto de. *O Brasil Anedótico.* Rio de Janeiro, 1941.
Carvalho, Affonso de. "Abolicionismo e democracia nas Arcadas," *Revista do Instituto Histórico e Geográfico de São Paulo,* XXXII, 353-367.
Codman, John. *Ten Months in Brazil.* Edinburgh, 1870.
Contribuições para a biográfia de D. Pedro II, Revista do Instituto Histórico e Geográfico Brasileiro. Special volume. Rio de Janeiro, 1925.
Courtin, René. *Le probleme de la civilization économique au Brésil.* Paris, 1941.
Cunha, Enclydes da. "Da independência à republica," *Revista do Instituto Histórico e Geográfico Brasileiro,* LXIX, Pt. 2, 7-71.
———. *Rebellion in the Backlands.* Translated by Samuel J. Putnam. Chicago, 1944.
Docea, Souza. *Causas da guerra com o paraguay.* Porto Alegre, 1919.
Domville-Fife, Charles W. *The United States of Brazil.* New York, n. d.
Duarte Filho, João. *O sertão e o centro.* 2nd ed.: Rio de Janeiro, 1939.
Duque-Estrada, Osorio. *A abolição.* Rio de Janeiro, 1918.
Fialho, Anfriso. *História da fundação da república no Brasil.* Rio de Janeiro, 1891.
Figueiredo, Lima. *Grandes solados do Brasil.* 2nd ed.: Rio de Janeiro, 1942.

Fletcher, Reverend James C., and Reverend D. P. Kidder. *Brazil and The Brazilians*. 9th ed.: Boston, 1879.

Fleiuss, Max. "D. Pedro II," *Revista do Instituto Histórico e Geográfico Brasileiro*, Tomo Especial (1925), v-xli.

————. *História administrativa do Brasil*. 2nd ed.: Rio de Janeiro, 1922.

Fonseca Filho, Hermes da. *Dois grandes vultos da república*. Porto Alegre, 1935.

Fontoura Castallat, General Bibiano Sergio Macado da. "Exercito," *Libro de Centenário, 1500-1900*. 2 vols. Rio de Janeiro, 1901.

Freyre, Gilberto. *O mundo que o Português criou*. Rio de Janeiro, 1940.

————. "Social Life in Brazil in the Middle of the Nineteenth Century," *Hispanic American Historical Review*, V, 597-630.

Galanti, P. Raphael M., S. J. *História do Brasil*. 5 vols. São Paulo, 1913.

Guanabara, Alcindo. *A presidencial Campos Salles*. Rio de Janeiro, 1902.

Handelmann, Henrique. *História do Brasil*. Brazilian translation by the Brazilian Institute of History and Geography. Rio de Janeiro, 1931.

Harding, Bertita. *Amazon Throne*. New York, 1941.

Hill, Lawrence F. "The Abolition of the African Slave Trade in Brazil," *Hispanic American Historical Review*, XIV, 167-196.

———— (ed.). *Brazil*. Berkeley, 1947.

Hilliard, Henry W. *Politics and Pen Pictures*. New York, 1892.

Ibiapina, J. de Mattos. *O Brasil de ontem e o de hoje*. Rio de Janeiro, 1942.

James, Herman G. *Brazil after a Century of Independence*. New York, 1925.

Lacombe, Americo Jacobina. "As ùltimas atitudes políticas de Saraiva," *Revista do Instituto Histórico e Geográfico Brasileiro*, CLXXXIV, 213-227.

Leal, Aurelino. *História constitucional do Brasil*. Rio de Janeiro, 1931.

Lellis, Alceu de. "O nordeste brasileiro," *Sociedade de Geografia do Rio de Janeiro, Geografia do Brasil*, I, 3-33.

Lima, Oliveira. *Formação histórica da nacionalidade brasileira*. Rio de Janeiro, 1944.

————. *O império brasileiro, 1822-1889*. São Paulo, 1927.

————. "Sept ans de republique au Brasil," *La Nouvelle Revue*, CI, 506-526.

"Luis Alvez de Lima e Silva, Duque de Caxias," *Encyclopédia e Dicionario Internacional*, IV. Rio de Janeiro, 1936.

Lyra, Tavares de. "Manoel Deodoro da Fonseca," *Revista do Instituto Histórico e Geográfico Brasileiro*, CLV, 274-297.

Manchester, Alan K. *British Preëminence in Brazil*. Chapel Hill, N. C., 1933.

"Manoel Mendes da Fonseca," *Encyclopedia e Dicionário Internacional,* VI. Rio de Janeiro, 1936.

"Marechal Manoel Deodoro da Fonseca," *Revista do Instituto Histórico e Geográfico Brasileiro,* LV, Pt. 2, 531-536.

Martin, Percy Alvin. "Causes of the Collapse of the Brazilian Empire," *Hispanic American Historical Review,* IV, 4-48.

————. "Slavery and Abolition in Brazil," *Hispanic American Historical Review,* XIII, 151-196.

Mattoso, Ernesto. *Causas do meu tempo.* Bordeaux, 1916.

Maximiliano, Carlos. *Comentários à constituição brasileira.* Porto Alegre, 1929.

Memezes, Djacir. *O Brasil econômico.* Rio de Janeiro, 1944.

Merou, Martin Garcia. *El Brasil intellectual.* Buenos Aires, 1944.

Moniz, Heitor. "Estadista do império," *Revista do Instituto Histórico e Geográfico Brasileiro,* CLI, 109-136.

Monteiro, Tobias. *História do império, o primeiro reinado.* 2 vols. Rio de Janeiro, 1946.

————. *Pesquisas e depoímentos para a história.* Rio de Janeiro, 1913.

————. "Reminiscencias do Almirante Saldanha," *Revista do Instituto Histórico e Geográfico Brasileiro,* CLXXXIV, 227-241.

Moraes, Evaristo de. "Pedro II e o movimento abolicionista," *Revista do Instituto Histórico e Geográfico Brasileiro.*

Mosse, Benjamin. *Dom Pedro II, Empereur du Brésil.* Paris, 1889.

Nabuco, Joaquim. *Minha formaçao.* Rio de Janeiro, 1934.

————. *Um estadista do império, Nabuco de Araujo, sua vida, suas opiniões, sua época.* 3 vols. Rio de Janeiro, 1896.

Normano, John F. *Brazil, A Study of Economic Types.* Chapel Hill, N. C., 1935.

————. "Brazil's Industrial Development," in *University of Miami Hispanic American Studies,* edited by Robert E. McNicoll and J. Riis Ouvre, Miami, 1947.

Oakenful, John C. *Brazil in 1911.* London, 1912.

Oliveiro, Colonel Antonio José de. "Guerra do Paraguay," *Revista do Instituto Histórico e Geográfico Brasileiro,* Dedicated to the first Congress of National History, Special volume, Pt. 5, pp. 297-365.

Ottoni, Counselor Carlos Honario Benedicto. *O advento da república no Brasil.* Rio de Janeiro, 1890.

Ouro Preto, Viscount de [Count d'Affonso Celso]. "Advento da dictadura militar no Brasil," *Revista do Instituto Histórico e Geofráfico Brasileiro,* LXCVI, 9-187.

————. *A marinha d'outrora.* Rio de Janeiro, 1894.

————. *Oito anos de parlamento.* Rio de Janeiro, 1901.

————. "Poder pessoal do imperador, inversão das situações politicas, os programas dos partidos, agitção democratica," *Revista do Instituto Histórico e Geográfico Brasileiro,* Dedicated to the first Congress of National History, Special volume, Pt. 5, pp. 378-412.

Pattee, Richard. "Portugal in America," in *University of Miami Hispanic American Studies*, edited by Robert E. McNicoll and J. Riis Ouvre. Miami, 1939.

Pereira da Silva, J. M. *Memórias do meu tempo*. 2 vols. Paris, 1896.

————. *Situation sociale, politique et économique de l'empire du Brésil*. Rio de Janeiro, 1912.

Prado Junior, Caio. *Formação do brasil contemporâneo*. 2nd ed.: São Paulo, 1945.

Pressoa, Paula. *Guia da cidade do Rio de Janeiro*. Rio de Janeiro, 1945.

Rebello, S. Velloso. *As primeiras tentativas da independência do Brasil*. Lisbon, 1915.

Ribas, Antonio Joaquim. *Perfil biográfico de Campos Salles*. Rio de Janeiro, 1896.

Rocha Pombo, José Francisco da. *História do Brasil*. 10 vols. Rio de Janeiro, n. d.

————. "A maioridade, desde quando se cogita da maioridade," *Revista do Instituto Histórico e Geográfico Brasileiro*, CLII, 218-223.

Roderigues, José Carlos. "Religiões acatólicas," *Libro de Centenario, 1500-1900*. 2 vols. Rio de Janeiro, 1901.

Sá Hornane Tavares de. *The Brazilians, People of Tomorrow*. New York, 1917.

Scully, William. *Brazil, Its Provinces and Chief Cities*. London, 1866.

Senna, Ernesto. *Deodoro, subsídios para a história*. Rio de Janeiro, 1896.

Setubal, Paulo. *As maluquices do imperador*. São Paulo, 1926.

Silveira Lobo, Francisco José da. "Ultimas dias da monarchia em São Paulo," *Revista do Instituto Histórico e Geográfico de São Paulo*, XXVII, 121-161.

Simoens, Silva da. "Um episódio do dio 15 de Novembro," *Revista do Instituto Histórico e Geográfico Brasileiro*, CXCIV, 127-131.

Simonsen, Robert C. *Brazil's Industrial Evolution*. São Paulo, 1931.

Smith, T. Lynn. *Brazil: People and Institutions*. Baton Rouge, 1947.

"Sobre o sanemento da Capital Federal," *Revista do Instituto Histórico e Geográfico Brasileiro*, LXXII, Pt. 2, 140-149.

Sousa, Octaviano Pereira de. "História do guerra do Paraguay," *Revista do Instituto Histórico e Geográfico Brasileiro*, CLVI, 8-93.

Tacito. "Ainda a ultima sessão do conselho d'estado," *Revista do Instituto Histórico e Geográfico de São Paulo*, VIII, 211-222.

Taunay, Viscount de. *O visconde de Rio Branco*. 2nd ed.: São Paulo, 1930.

"Tracos biográficos de D. Pedro II," *Revista do Instituto Histórico e Geógráfico Brasileiro*, CLII, 111-187.

Turner, Charles W. *Ruy Barbosa*. New York, 1945.

Vianna, Oliveira. *O Occaso do império*. São Paulo, 1925.

————. "A queda do império," in *Contribuições para a Biografia de D. Pedro II, Revista do Instituto Histórico e Geográfico Brasileiro*. Tomo Especial. Rio de Janeiro, 1925.

Visconde de Ouro Preto (Exerptos biográficos), *Revista do Instituto Histórico e Geográfico Brasileiro*, CLVII, 7-570.

Walsh, R. *Notices of Brazil in 1828 and 1829*. 2 vols. London, 1830.

Washburn, Charles A. *The History of Paraguay*. 2 vols. Boston, 1871.

Wells, James W. *Three Thousand Miles Through Brazil*. 2 vols. London, 1887.

Williams, Mary Wilhelmine. *Dom Pedro the Magnanimous*. Chapel Hill, N. C., 1937.

-◄[Index]►-